DESMOND DOSS
CONSCIENTIOUS OBJECTOR

THE STORY OF AN UNLIKELY HERO

FRANCES M. DOSS

Pacific Press®
Publishing Association
Nampa, Idaho | Oshawa, Ontario, Canada
www.pacificpress.com

D1291035

Design by Dennis Ferree
Cover photo by John LeMay

Copyright © 2005 by
Pacific Press® Publishing Association
Printed in the United States of America

Additional copies of this book are available by calling toll-free
1-800-765-6955 or by visiting www.adventistbookcenter.com

Library of Congress Cataloging-in-Publication Data
Doss, Frances M. (Frances May) 1922-
Desmond Doss : conscientious objector : the story of an unlikely hero /
Frances M. Doss
p. cm.
ISBN 978-0-8163-2124-7
1. Doss, Desmond. 2. World War, 1939-1945—Conscientious
objectors—United States—Biography. 3. United States. Army—
Medical personnel—Biography. 4. World War, 1939-1945—
Medical care—United States. 5. United States. Army—Sanitary
affairs. 6. Medal of Honor. I. Title.

D810.C82D68 2005
940.54'7573092—dc22
[B]
2005054430

July 2016

DEDICATION

Because Desmond's mother always meant so much to him,
I wish to dedicate this little book to the memory of
Mrs. Bertha Doss

And because my own mother always meant so much to me,
I wish also to dedicate this little book to the memory of
Mrs. Gertrude Sherman

In appreciation
Frances Doss

The President of the United States
in the name of The Congress
takes pleasure in presenting the
Medal of Honor
to

DOSS, DESMOND T.

Rank and organization: Private First Class, U.S. Army, Medical Detachment, 307th Infantry, 77th Infantry Division. *Place and date:* Near Urasoe Mura, Okinawa, Ryukyu Islands, 29 April-21 May 1945. *Entered service at:* Lynchburg, Va. *Birth:* Lynchburg, Va. *G.O. No.:* 97, 1 November 1945.

Citation: He was a company aid man when the 1st Battalion assaulted a jagged escarpment 400 feet high. As our troops gained the summit, a heavy concentration of artillery, mortar and machinegun fire crashed into them, inflicting approximately 75 casualties and driving the others back. Pfc. Doss refused to seek cover and remained in the fire-swept area with the many stricken, carrying them 1 by 1 to the edge of the escarpment and there lowering them on a rope-supported litter down the face of a cliff to friendly hands. On 2 May, he exposed himself to heavy rifle and mortar fire in rescuing a wounded man 200 yards forward of the lines on the same escarpment; and 2 days later he treated 4 men who had been cut down while assaulting a strongly defended cave, advancing through a shower of grenades to within 8 yards of enemy forces in a cave's mouth, where he dressed his comrades' wounds before making 4 separate trips under fire to evacuate them to safety. On 5 May, he unhesitatingly braved enemy shelling and small arms fire to assist an artillery officer. He applied bandages, moved his patient to a spot that offered protection from small arms fire and, while artillery and mortar shells fell close by, painstakingly adminis-

DESMOND DOSS

tered plasma. Later that day, when an American was severely wounded by fire from a cave, Pfc. Doss crawled to him where he had fallen 25 feet from the enemy position, rendered aid, and carried him 100 yards to safety while continually exposed to enemy fire. On 21 May, in a night attack on high ground near Shuri, he remained in exposed territory while the rest of his company took cover, fearlessly risking the chance that he would be mistaken for an infiltrating Japanese and giving aid to the injured until he was himself seriously wounded in the legs by the explosion of a grenade. Rather than call another aid man from cover, he cared for his own injuries and waited 5 hours before litter bearers reached him and started carrying him to cover. The trio was caught in an enemy tank attack and Pfc. Doss, seeing a more critically wounded man nearby, crawled off the litter; and directed the bearers to give their first attention to the other man. Awaiting the litter bearers' return, he was again struck, this time suffering a compound fracture of 1 arm. With magnificent fortitude he bound a rifle stock to his shattered arm as a splint and then crawled 300 yards over rough terrain to the aid station. Through his outstanding bravery and unflinching determination in the face of desperately dangerous conditions Pfc. Doss saved the lives of many soldiers. His name became a symbol throughout the 77th Infantry Division for outstanding gallantry far above and beyond the call of duty.

October 12, 1945
THE WHITE HOUSE

DESMOND'S FAVORITES

Bible text:

"Trust in the LORD with all thine heart; and lean not unto thine own understanding. In all thy ways acknowledge him, and he shall direct thy paths" (Proverbs 3:5, 6).

Salutation:

God bless you.

Sayings:

"Anything that's not worth doing right to start with is not worth doing at all."

"It's not how much you know, but what you do with what you know."

PREFACE

Dear Reader:

The reason I asked Frances, my godly wife, to write this book for me is that she knows more than anyone else about my God-given experiences and my desire to stick to the facts as much as possible.

My main interest is to encourage you, our readers, to choose to dedicate your lives to the Lord and be ready to meet Him at His soon return.

God wrote the Ten Commandments on tables of stone with His own finger. He said it was perfect and that nothing is to be added to it or taken away from it. We are to be judged by this law of liberty, so whether we accept or reject it is a matter of life or death.

Frances and I have dedicated our lives to Christ and have given Him first place in our hearts. As a result He has given us a greater love for each other than we ever thought possible, and we have never been happier.

Sincerely, your Christian brother in Christ,
Desmond T. Doss, CMH

CONTENTS

CHAPTER ONE

MEMORIES—I

The lone soldier was standing by the rail of the troop ship, looking out over the ocean. A beautiful half moon hung in the western sky, its silver trail shining across the water. The soldier was on a troop ship leaving Hawaii, where the 77th Infantry Division of the United States Army had been in jungle combat training. This was during World War II, and the soldiers on the ship knew they were heading west into the Pacific, but their destination was a secret—to them.

A few other soldiers wandered around on the dark deck—dark because a light could help enemy ships find them and send explosives in their direction. But in spite of the other men around him, Desmond felt quite alone up on the deck, and lonely, too. His thoughts went back to home and loved ones—his parents, his brother and sister, and his beautiful wife of two years. He missed Dorothy and remembered his last few moments with her before he had shipped out. When would he see her again? Would he see her again? The thought was so painful, he tried to turn his thoughts in another direction.

★ ★ ★ ★ ★

"This is a nice picture. What am I bid?" the auctioneer asked as he picked up another picture from the stack. "What am I bid?" he repeated. "Ten cents. I have ten cents. Who will make it twenty cents? OK, Mr. Brown. Thank you. I have twenty. Anyone make it fifty cents? It's worth much more—a beautiful picture. Fifty cents. Who will make it seventy-five?" He looked around. "There, I have seventy-five. Now, how about eighty cents?" He waited a few seconds before crying out, "Seventy-five, seventy-five, seventy-five. Anyone eighty? No? Going, going, gone at seventy-five cents to that man right over there."

"Oh, Mr. Doss. You've got yourself a bargain, Mr. Doss."

Mr. Thomas Doss took the picture in his hands, looked at it, and wondered why he had bid on an illustration of the Lord's Prayer and the Ten Commandments. He had to admit it was a very nice picture, but why did he want it?

"Oh, well," he muttered to himself, "Bertha will probably like it to hang on the wall in the living room." He had come to the auction to find furniture and other items for his new home. Thomas and Bertha hadn't been married long, and they were trying to furnish their small home without spending too much money.

Of course, this event had happened a number of years before Desmond Doss was born, but he had heard it many times. Besides, that picture was hanging on the living room wall at the little house on Easley Avenue right now. From the time he was a small boy, Desmond had looked at the picture many times. In fact, Mother Doss sometimes wished he weren't quite so interested in the picture—not because she didn't want him to look at it, but because he was always dragging a kitchen chair into the living room to stand on so that he could see the picture better.

One time she told him, "Desmond, please take the chair back to the kitchen, won't you? I declare, that chair seat is getting worn out, you stand on it so much." But Desmond could tell she wasn't really unhappy with him.

Standing on deck of a troop ship out on the Pacific Ocean and thinking about his life since childhood, he realized once again how much that picture had influenced his life. The sixth commandment, "Thou shalt not kill," was illustrated by a picture of Cain, with a club in his hands, standing over the dead body of his brother, Abel, just after killing him. Desmond often wondered, *How could a brother do such a thing?* It gave him such a horror of killing anybody or anything; he was sure the picture had made him decide to be a medical soldier who would save life instead of taking it. He could imagine Jesus saying to him, "Desmond, if you love Me, you will not kill, but save life as I would if I were in your place. Follow My example."

MEMORIES—I

His thoughts rambled on. Mother, bless her heart, always took her three children to Sabbath School and church services. First, she pushed Audrey to church in the baby carriage; later as Audrey walked beside her mother, Desmond occupied the baby carriage. Still later, Harold would ride in the carriage while the two other children skipped happily beside their mother.

"Desmond! Harold! It's time to study our Sabbath School lesson." Audrey already had her small Bible, ready to open it, and the boys soon joined her and Mother. It became a habit with them. Desmond recalled that when he was drafted into the army, he had just received his eight-year ribbon from the Sabbath School for attending each week, being on time, and studying his lesson seven times—once each day throughout the week.

Another memory was of attending the little church school in the back of the church on Park Avenue. Each pupil at the church school acted as a janitor. The teacher assigned various cleanup jobs to each student, changing the jobs from time to time so the children wouldn't be bored. Desmond well remembered one job he was told to do. He was to clean the blackboards and dust the erasers.

Now, that blackboard is OK, he thought to himself. *I'll take these erasers out and dust them, and then I can go home.* Then an idea popped into his head. He knew enough about erasers to know that if you rub them together, they will look clean—and you don't make all that dust that sticks in your throat and makes you cough. Besides, it would take less time. So Desmond rubbed the erasers together, took them back inside, and set them up on the blackboard—looking all clean, but filled with chalk dust.

The wise teacher, Nell Ketterman, came over to the blackboard just as Desmond set the erasers down. She picked up two and banged them together. You know what happened—the dust FLEW! Then she made a remark that Desmond had never forgotten. "Desmond, anything that's not worth doing right to start with isn't worth doing at all."

Desmond went out and dusted the erasers again—properly, this time. But what she said had stuck with him all his life. How many times that saying had come back to him as he grew up and after he was in the army. And how many times he had determined to do the job right the first time.

Shortly after that, Nell Ketterman had gone to China as a missionary. As Desmond was growing up, he thought he would like to be a missionary to some far-off place, just like his favorite teacher. He didn't realize it right then on that troop ship, but he would have a chance to be a missionary to people on the islands he was going to—at Uncle Sam's expense—because he would sometimes take care of the native islanders as well as the soldiers.

★ ★ ★ ★ ★

His next thought was of how God had taken care of him. Desmond seemed to be accident prone, and his mother wondered at times how he ever lived to grow up. To tell the truth, from his vantage point of twenty-five years of age, he sometimes wondered the same thing himself.

"Desmond, I need some milk or we won't have any for breakfast," said Mother Doss. "Run over to Aunt Ella's and get us a quart, will you?"

Aunt Ella grew a garden and also had a cow, and she very generously shared produce and milk with her relatives during this depression time. That was the reason Desmond was to go to Aunt Ella's for milk.

He could almost remember the conversation that usually went on between him and his aunt.

"Will one quart be enough, Desmond?" she would ask.

"That is all Mom said to get," Desmond would reply.

"All right." And Aunt Ella would pour the milk into the quart milk bottle that Desmond had brought. This was when milk came in glass bottles, not the plastic containers we see today.

"Thanks, Aunt Ella," and Desmond would be on his way, after promising to tell his mother hello for Aunt Ella.

But on this day Desmond never arrived at his aunt's house. He had to cross a cobblestone street on the way—better than mud but very bumpy. His foot tripped on one of the stones, and he fell. He didn't want to break the empty milk bottle he was carrying, so he tried to hold it up as he fell. It didn't work. The bottle broke!

He screamed as he fell, and neighbors heard him and came out to see who was hurt. Then someone ran to tell his mother. Mother, running out the door and down the sidewalk, found Desmond lying in the street.

"Desmond, honey, what have you done to yourself?" It took her only seconds to realize that his left hand was badly cut. She ran back into the house and got a large towel to wrap his hand in. One of the neighbors offered the use of his car to take Desmond to the Lynchburg hospital, to what we would now call the emergency room.

The doctor worked hard on the hand and then stitched it up. "Mrs. Doss, I've done the best I can, but I'm afraid your boy will never be able to use that hand again. With that tendon and those muscles being cut . . ." He didn't finish the sentence.

So Desmond was taken home with that dire prediction hanging over his head, and also over the head of his loving, but sad, mother. She couldn't stand to do nothing about it, so as soon as Desmond's hand began to heal and wasn't too sore to touch, she started working his fingers up and down, back and forth—stretching them out as far as they would go.

"Ow, Mom, that hurts!"

"Yes, son, I know, but we want to give that hand every chance to heal. See if you can move those fingers yourself when I'm not around to do it for you. And, Desmond, let's pray that God will heal your hand, shall we?" They had already prayed about it, but now they prayed even more earnestly.

"Mom, come here. I want to show you something," Desmond called to his mother as she came in the door a few days later from her work at the shoe factory.

"Yes, Desmond, what is it?" When Mother reached him, he held up his left hand—and wiggled the second finger.

"Desmond, how wonderful! You can move it!" exclaimed Mother. There was no doubt about her joy and happiness at this wonderful turn of events. "Let's say a little prayer right now and thank God for helping your hand." Desmond bowed his head as his mother thanked God for this wonderful blessing. His hand did heal, and although it didn't look quite the same as his right hand, he could use it, and he was glad.

★ ★ ★ ★ ★

As he stood on the deck that night, Desmond thought of another experience when God had blessed him in a very special way.

He had been out playing with the neighborhood children. They were running back and forth on the top of a rock wall. Desmond slipped and skinned his knee on the side of the rock wall as he fell. He remembered how it hurt. "I'm heading for home," he told the others.

"Oh, it hurts," he said to himself when he looked at it that night. But it would heal, and he didn't want to worry his mother over a little thing like a skinned knee. He tried to keep from limping and managed to hide the hurt from his family—for a couple of days, that is. On the third morning, he couldn't make himself get out of bed.

Mother had to go to work at the shoe factory, and she always left early. A neighbor lady, whom the children called Aunt Jenny, would come in, get the children up, give them their breakfast, and then see that they got off to school. That particular morning, she told Desmond it was time to get up, but noticed a few minutes later that he was still in bed. So she went to investigate.

She found him groaning and holding his knee. Even as inexperienced as she was medically, she could tell when she looked at his knee that he was in bad shape. The knee was red and hot, and ugly red streaks radiated from the bruise, indicating blood poisoning. This neighbor called Mother Doss at the shoe factory and told her to come home, explaining a little bit about Desmond's knee.

"Desmond, why didn't you tell me?" Mother asked when she had looked at the knee herself.

"I thought it would heal up and be OK; I didn't want to worry you." Mother thought to herself that it would have been better to have worried her a couple of days earlier than waiting until now, but she didn't remind Desmond of that right then.

Of course, the doctor came. After examining the knee carefully, he told the parents, for Father had arrived by that time, "I hate to tell you this, but you can see his knee is badly infected, and I can see nothing to do except to amputate the leg. The poison from the infection is getting into his body and could kill him."

Kill him! What a thought! But how could they allow the doctor to cut off one of Desmond's legs! No! No! Have Desmond get around with just one leg? That would be terrible. But if they didn't and Desmond died? What a decision to make!

"Doctor, isn't there anything we can do?" asked Mother Doss desperately. The doctor suggested it might help if she put a hot pack on the knee.

"It won't hurt to try, Mrs. Doss, but you will have to do it at least every two hours, and I wonder if it will help. Try it, but if it isn't somewhat better by tomorrow, the leg will have to come off," replied the doctor as he left.

Mother put a large pan of hot water on the stove and kept it hot. Then she wrung out a big towel and put it around Desmond's knee, then covered it with a heavy folded towel to keep the heat in. She changed the towel to a new, hot one often.

Of course, as she was doing this, she was also praying that God would bless her efforts and save Desmond's leg. After putting the hot packs on his knee for the rest of that day and then all night long, Mother Doss was exhausted, but she would not give up.

"Mom, it doesn't hurt as much as it did," Desmond remarked during the night. As his mother carefully examined the knee again, she felt it didn't look quite as bad, either. The red streaks seemed to be fading away. With tears of gratitude in her eyes, she thanked the Lord, continued to pray—and kept changing hot packs.

When the doctor came the next day, he examined the knee again. "Mrs. Doss, I really think you're winning the battle. We'll watch the knee very carefully for the next couple of days, but it seems to be better." Welcome words! The whole family rejoiced but none more than Desmond.

He remembered one other thing about that experience. After lying in bed for several days and getting all those treatments and knowing his leg was better, he decided he wanted to get up, so he sat on the edge of the bed, put his feet down, stood up—and sprawled on the floor! He found he had to get his strength back and almost learn to walk all over again.

★ ★ ★ ★ ★

He remembered yet one other time as he stood on the ship's deck that night, leaning on the rail. This time the memory didn't revolve around himself.

Desmond's brother, Harold, was sick—very sick. His temperature was up to 103 degrees, and he was in a lot of pain. Mother had done all she knew to do for him, but it didn't seem to help. He was still hot and groaning in pain. The doctor had come, but he was at a loss to know what to do for Harold.

"Mrs. Doss, I wonder if he will live through the night. If he does, I'll bring another doctor with me tomorrow morning, and we'll take a spinal tap to see if we can decide where the problem is and whether we can help him." The doctor's words weren't very comforting.

"Desmond, I believe we should pray for Harold, don't you?" Mother Doss said to her older son.

"Yes, Mom, I think we should. Will Jesus make Harold well?" asked Desmond.

"We don't know for sure, honey. We always want to ask that God's will be done. But we can always ask." So mother and son knelt beside the sick boy's bed, and Mother prayed, "Dear Father in heaven, You know that Harold is very sick, and You know he is in a lot of pain. Would You please bring healing to his body if that can be according to Your will? But if You see that it is best not to heal him . . . " Her voice broke with a sob at this point, "then please bring the end soon so that he will not have to suffer so much. Thank You, Lord. Amen."

As Mother and Desmond rose from their knees, they glanced at Harold. They suddenly realized he was not breathing as hard as he had been. The thought came to them that he was dying, but NO! He was breathing quietly, and the color was coming back into his pale face. Soon he fell into a peaceful sleep and woke up the next morning feeling very good. How could Desmond ever forget that experience!

The doctor came the next morning as he promised and was very much surprised to see Harold doing so well. Mother just had to tell the doctor about her prayer and how Harold had improved right away.

"Son," he said to Harold, "the Lord has saved your life, and I trust it is for a good purpose."

★ ★ ★ ★ ★

I'm getting tired. Think I will turn in and get some shut-eye, Desmond thought as he made his way to his bunk. Soon he was asleep.

CHAPTER TWO

MEMORIES—II

A couple of nights later Desmond again found his way to the deck of the troop ship. The moon was a little higher in the sky, its trail still shining across the water to the ship. His recollections continued.

★ ★ ★ ★ ★

"Wish I had a bike," Desmond remarked to his friend Paul. "Then we could go for a bike ride together."

"Why don't you get one?" asked Paul.

"Can't. No money." It was quiet for a moment, but only a moment. Paul came up with an idea.

"Let's go to the dump. Sometimes there are bicycle parts there that people have thrown away. We can make a bike for you! Let's go!"

Desmond was agreeable, and before long the boys were at the city dump, seeing what they could find.

"Here's a bicycle frame, I think," said Paul, as he dug around in the trash. "Yes, it is! Doesn't look too bad, either."

"And here is a wheel. No—two wheels!" Desmond was as excited as Paul.

They scrounged around and found a sprocket, two or three chains in case they didn't have the right size, and even two old tires that looked like they would need patching, but maybe they could manage that. They even found front and back fenders—one was blue and one was red, but they would do.

DESMOND DOSS

The boys went home, dragging their treasures behind them. They found some bolts and screws in Paul's dad's toolbox, and soon they had put a bicycle together. It didn't look like much, but it worked—and that was the main thing. Desmond and Paul took many bike rides together and probably enjoyed and appreciated them all the more because of the work they had done on the old bike.

But Desmond remembered that the bicycle had gotten him into trouble a few times too. After he got the bike, he rode it to school every day. One day he started for school. As he passed Green's Grocery, he noticed Mr. Woods's dairy delivery truck. One of those daredevil ideas came to him! Why not hang on to the truck and ride? It would even help him get to school early.

So, when Mr. Woods jumped in the truck to make the run to his next delivery stop, Desmond grabbed the right rear fender and hung on.

This is really fun! he thought, as the truck pulled out onto Campbell Avenue, a nicely paved main road in Lynchburg. There wasn't a lot of traffic at that time in the morning. "This is fun; it isn't even dangerous!" Desmond said out loud. Once in a while the truck swerved over toward the curb, leaving very little room between the truck and the curb. Obviously, Mr. Woods didn't realize he had a boy hanging on to the back of his truck. Desmond began to realize this could be dangerous after all!

Then he looked ahead to the bottom of the hill and saw the railroad tracks they would cross. Two sets of tracks and also the streetcar tracks that turned the corner at that intersection. Desmond cringed a little but hung on; he was going too fast now to let go.

It was a bumpy ride across the tracks. He wondered momentarily if his old bike could take the punishment. When the bike hit the tracks, it seemed like the wheels might come to pieces, and two or three times he felt he was losing control and would surely be thrown off the bicycle. But the truck soon crossed all of the tracks and then rolled smoothly up the hill to the next delivery stop.

Boylike and daredevil-like, Desmond had almost forgotten the danger by the time Mr. Woods stopped his truck at the restaurant to deliver milk and other dairy products. Mr. Woods jumped out of the truck and came around to the back to get out the things he needed to deliver.

"Thanks for the buggy ride." Mr. Woods looked around as he heard Desmond's voice. He suddenly realized what this boy meant by "buggy ride." His face went white.

"Boy, don't you know you could have been killed? Don't ever do that again."

Desmond couldn't say anything but "OK," but it was a rather shame-faced boy who jumped on his bike and started for school at a more leisurely pace.

★ ★ ★ ★ ★

Another memory involved a time that was even more daredevilish and dangerous.

Lynchburg was a crossroad for trains. The big, old steam engines with their long lines of freight cars and the engines pulling passenger cars always fascinated the boys who lived near the tracks. Mothers in the neighborhood didn't like the noise and didn't appreciate the black smoke and cinders that covered the area, but the boys didn't worry about such things.

School was out for the day, and Desmond and his cousins, Preston and Beverly (that really was his name), were wondering what interesting thing they could do before they needed to run home for supper.

"I know," said Preston. "Let's go down to the Twelfth Street station and see Dad's train go through. I think it goes through about now." Preston's father was a conductor on the passenger train.

"OK, let's go," agreed Desmond and Beverly.

When they reached the station, the train had just pulled in for a short stop. Desmond's Uncle Lanza jumped off the train, helped a couple of passengers down, then swung back up on the train and motioned the engineer to go on. He saw the three boys watching the train and waved to them as the train picked up speed.

When the passenger train had gone on, a long freight train that had been shunted to the side while the passenger train went by started to move down the tracks, very slowly at first.

Just then another of those daredevilish ideas popped into Desmond's brain.

"Hey, let's hop the train!" he yelled above its noise.

"Ain't that dangerous?" asked Beverly as he looked at the freight cars rumbling by.

"Naw. My dad used to do that when he went to visit my mom before they got married. Called it grabbing the arm of freight. He did it all the time. Just jump up and grab on to the ladders that go up the side. Easy!" Of course, Desmond didn't have time to mention that Dad worked on the railroad and knew just how to jump on and get off. Or that the train was usually going pretty slow.

Preston and Beverly seemed to be convinced, so they all started running along beside the train, not thinking how dangerous Desmond's idea was.

"I'll go first and show you how," yelled Desmond, as he proceeded to grab on to the ladder. The other two followed his example, and they were "riding the train."

Preston and Beverly soon had enough and dropped off, but not Desmond.

"Desmond, jump off! It's going faster," both boys screamed.

"It's too fast!! I can't jump off now!" he said. But his mind told him he had to get off the train before it went on the trestle over Campbell Avenue. He finally did let go and hit the ground, rolling down the embankment and up against the concrete wall that separated the bank from Campbell Avenue thirty or thirty-five feet below. Ten more seconds, and he would have been splashed on the street—very dead.

"Wow. That was close!" He was breathing hard from the effort and excitement of jumping off. He gingerly moved his arms and legs. They worked OK! He knew there would be a few bruises, but at least no broken bones.

He sort of limped home and stayed out of sight when his mother came in from her work at the shoe factory. She noticed he was a little bit quiet, but she had to get supper on the table. She would talk to him later.

He didn't want his father—who used to ride the trains to see his mother—to find out about what he had done, but just as his father came in the door, the phone rang and Dad answered it.

"What? What are you telling me?" he said as he glanced over in Desmond's direction. He listened for a few moments longer and then hung up. Desmond found out later that his cousins hadn't seen him jump off the train and had reported the whole episode to Aunt Maud, who called to find out if Desmond was home and if he was hurt.

"Desmond, what on earth do you think you were doing? I just heard about it. You're crazy to think you can hop a train. I'll teach you not to do such things." Dad was not a Christian at that time, and he had a fiery, uncontrolled temper; it was definitely uncontrolled at that moment.

"Dad, I won't do it again! I mean it. I'll never do it again!"

"I know you won't do it again. I'll make sure you won't!" Angrily, Mr. Doss pulled off his wide leather belt and started to beat his son. Desmond screamed as the belt hit his back and legs and other parts of his anatomy. He thought Dad would never stop! Blood was beginning to flow as the belt hit his back. It was hurting so bad—he almost wished he had been killed when he jumped off the train!

Mother still didn't really know what it was all about, but she came to the rescue. "Thomas, that's enough! You've beat him too hard already."

"Well, he deserves it. Dumb kid!" Dad's anger was vented, and he stomped off into the other room.

"Desmond, what on earth did you do to deserve that?" said Mother as she knelt beside him. And Desmond, between sobs, confessed how he had jumped on the train.

"Oh, Son. Don't you know you could have been killed doing that? You could have fallen so easily and even had your feet cut off under those train wheels."

"Yes, I do now, Mom. I won't ever try that again."

"I'm glad to hear you say that, honey. I sure wouldn't want to lose my boy that way. And when you promise me, I know you'll keep that promise." Mother was a wise woman and knew that showing confidence in her son would help him more than scolding, to do what he should do. On the deck that night, Desmond couldn't help but remember that experience, and as he thought of it, he realized anew that God had protected that "dumb kid" again, and that he had much to be thankful for.

Another thought crossed his mind as it had whenever he remembered that experience. What if Preston or Beverly had fallen from the train and been killed or had lost a foot or a leg? It would have been his—Desmond's—fault. He couldn't help but realize how important it was to set a good example. In fact, it had made such an impression on his mind even when it happened that it really had helped him to try to set a good example a number of times.

As he thought about these things, he wondered how much these experiences had to do with decisions he made when he grew up and especially when he got into the army. Things like the Ten Commandments picture and how it showed him what was right and wrong, and his mother's influence and her wise way of helping him see what would make him grow into a kind, thoughtful, and helpful young man; a young man who would stand for the right no matter what, and remember the importance of setting a good example.

There wasn't much to do aboard ship as the big troop transport carried the soldiers to their destination. Desmond felt weary and soon found his way to his bunk.

CHAPTER THREE

MEMORIES—III

A few nights out from Hawaii, Desmond again found "his spot" on the deck of the ship. He had been thinking of some of the near tragedies in his younger life. Now his thoughts took a little different direction.

★ ★ ★ ★ ★

He remembered that his mother was a hard and faithful worker, and her bosses at the shoe factory appreciated her work. She was faithful, too, in giving the Lord what belonged to Him. More than once he had heard her remark, "I surely wouldn't rob a bank, and I'm not going to rob God," referring to paying tithe from her income—the 10 percent that God says belongs to Him.

But God also promises a special blessing to those who are faithful in giving to Him the tithe. God doesn't ask people to pay tithe to make it hard on them; it gives Him a chance to bless them. People who pay tithe have found that nine-tenths goes further than ten-tenths. Desmond remembered a couple of times when God did bless them as Mother said He would.

After living in several different houses in Lynchburg, the Dosses had the chance to buy a small house on Easley Avenue from Mr. Vandergrift, a Seventh-day Adventist friend. He and his wife had several children and needed a bigger home. So the Dosses made a small down payment and arranged to make monthly payments on the house.

"The house payment isn't very much," Mother Doss remarked to her husband one day, "but with you working only once in a while at an odd job, and me not having full-time work at the factory, I don't see how we are going to make even the small monthly payment on the house this month."

"I sure hope Mr. Vandergrift won't be too hard on us, but he has a family and needs the money too," replied Mr. Doss.

"Well, I'm going to be sure to pray about it," Mrs. Doss said.

"Don't know as it will do any good," said her husband rather gruffly, "but go ahead. Won't hurt." Mother Doss remembered, too, that God had promised to give that special blessing to those who were faithful in paying tithe, so when she prayed, she asked God for the special blessing they needed right now.

A couple of days later there was a knock at the door. Desmond went to open it, and there stood Mr. Vandergrift. Desmond knew about the house payment problem, so he wondered what the man wanted, but he invited him in.

"Mom, Mr. Vandergrift is here," he told his mother when he found her in the kitchen.

"Oh, hello, Mr. Vandergrift. Won't you sit down?" she said as she came into the living room.

"Thanks, Mrs. Doss. I came to talk to you about the house payment." Mother wondered what he would say about the payment that wasn't quite due, but would be in two more days.

"I know you folks have been having a pretty hard time lately, and I'm quite sure you are having a hard time scraping up enough money to give me the house payment. Isn't that true?"

"Yes, Mr. Vandergrift, it is true. We have some of it but not all."

"I'd like to propose something. Would you be able to pay just half the payment for a few months until things are better for you?" he asked.

"Mr. Vandergrift, that would be an answer to my prayers. It's been worrying me, and I have been praying about it," Mother Doss admitted. "I have the half I can give you right now."

So saying, she did just that, and when Mr. Vandergrift left, he left a very happy and thankful family behind him. It made a deep impression on the mind of young Desmond too.

He remembered that things did get better and that they were soon able to resume full payments. They even managed to pay a little extra at times, and the very last payment was made one month before it was due. Mother always did say it was because she gave God what was His first— the tithe.

Oh, yes, there had been one more time when they saw that special blessing from God. Green's Grocery gave credit to customers unless they got too far behind in their payments. Then Mr. Green would regretfully cut them off.

One night, Desmond remembered, he and his folks and Harold and Audrey went down to Green's Grocery to get a few things and to pay something on the grocery bill. When they brought the things to the counter, Mr. Green asked kindly, "Mrs. Doss, I've noticed you haven't been buying so many groceries lately. Is something wrong?"

"Well, Mr. Green, we've been going down to the supermarket and buying some things there. They are a little cheaper, and we thought by doing that we could have a little more to pay on our grocery bill to you. I know it is quite high," she said rather timidly. "I do appreciate you not cutting us off."

"Mrs. Doss, your credit here is good just as long as this store stays open," he replied. Desmond knew of others, even some of his relatives, who were having to pay cash for their groceries, so he realized this was a blessing.

Of course that made Mother Doss very happy, not only because she wouldn't have to worry quite so much about the grocery bill, but because of the confidence Mr. Green expressed in her. Again, she knew God had given them that special blessing because she had been faithful in paying her tithe.

★ ★ ★ ★ ★

Once more Desmond's thoughts moved to other memories.

How could he forget the night his father got drunk? The Doss family had gone over to visit Aunt Mattie, father's sister, and her husband, Uncle Arthur. While the children were playing together and the ladies were visiting, Dad and Uncle Arthur started to drink from the bottles Uncle Arthur brought out.

Now Mother Doss had laid down the law to Thomas about drinking. "Thomas," she said, "you took me from a good home where there was no drinking, and I don't like this drinking you are doing. I have three children to raise, and I won't have you drinking around them or bringing drink into our home. You either leave the drink alone, or you can leave us." Father knew she meant every word she said, and since he really did love her and his family, he decided to stop drinking.

He had been doing really well. But when he and Uncle Arthur got together that night, he forgot about his decision not to drink. It wasn't long before they were both just drunk enough to want to fight.

Who remembers what they were fighting about? Later, they certainly couldn't remember. The family was watching what went on, and to Mother Doss's surprise, Daddy Doss pulled out a pistol and pointed it at Uncle Arthur.

"Thomas, stop that!" she screamed at him.

Neither of the men was so drunk that he didn't realize that Mother Doss had stepped between them, and surely neither of them wanted to see Mother hurt. Aunt Mattie went to the phone and called the police.

"Thomas, give me that gun! The police are coming, and you know how hard it will go for you if they find you with a gun." Mother Doss held out her hand. Thomas knew what she said was true, so he handed her the gun. She stepped out from between the men then.

She handed the gun to Desmond. "Go hide it, Desmond. I don't care where."

Desmond ran home with the gun. As he entered the house, he wondered where a good hiding place would be where his father couldn't find it.

"Oh, I know. How about that big pitcher where Mom keeps her crocheting?" He dumped the crocheting on the table, put the gun in the bottom of the pitcher, and then put the crocheting back into the pitcher. Later Desmond told his mother where the gun was. It stayed there for some time until Mother Doss finally hid it at the bottom of a drawer that was seldom used.

After hiding the gun, Desmond ran back to his uncle's house just in time to see his daddy being hauled away in the "Black Maria," the vehicle used to transport drunks and others. Daddy stayed in jail for a day until he got sobered up. He decided Bertha was right in telling him not to drink.

The one thing that this experience did for Desmond was to put into his mind and heart a great determination not to drink or smoke. He could see the awful things such habits could do to people. He remembered now that two of his uncles had died as a result of smoking. He was never sorry for the decision he made that day never to drink alcohol or to smoke.

★ ★ ★ ★ ★

Once more, a tired Desmond found his way to his bunk, and after kneeling quietly for prayer, he crawled in. For just a moment before he went to sleep he remembered that at one time his fellow soldiers had thrown a few shoes and boots at him when he prayed, but they were used to his habits by now and didn't bother him. He was soon asleep.

CHAPTER FOUR

MEMORIES—IV

The little corner of the troop ship deck seemed almost like home to him now. It was one place where he could get away from the bustle of the many soldiers aboard ship and think a little.

The sun had not quite set as Desmond settled down on his box that night. He pulled from his pocket the little Bible Dorothy had given him shortly after they were married. First he read the Bible verse she had written in the flyleaf, "There hath no temptation taken you but such as is common to man: but God is faithful, who will not suffer you to be tempted above that ye are able; but will with the temptation also make a way of escape, that ye may be able to bear it" (1 Corinthians 10:13). He read other texts that gave him a sense of help and encouragement. Then he prayed a little prayer—for his parents, his wife, and himself. He felt they needed prayer, and he knew he did.

★ ★ ★ ★ ★

Now he was thinking of something that had brought joy to his life.

At the time his mother had studied the Bible and decided to follow its teachings and become a Seventh-day Adventist, his father was also interested in the Bible and what she was studying. But work was scarce during the depression, and he knew that asking for Sabbaths off would make it even harder to get a job.

"If I became a Seventh-day Adventist, we'd starve," was his excuse. So through the years he stayed away from church. Also he continued to smoke, a practice not permitted to members of the Seventh-day Adventist

Church. After the night when he and his brother-in-law got in a fight, he decided there would be no more drinking for him.

Sometime later Thomas and Bertha were discussing some meetings being held at Buena Vista, approximately twenty miles from Lynchburg. "I'd really like to go," said Bertha. "Could we at least go over there for the Friday night meeting? I hear Elder Lester Coon is a good speaker."

"Doesn't sound bad. OK, let's go," her husband agreed.

Audrey, Desmond, and Harold were delighted. They didn't very often get away from Lynchburg, so this would be a real treat for them. It was Friday afternoon when they all piled into the family car to go to Buena Vista.

Thinking of that car reminded Desmond of the time Jack, their pet English bulldog, rammed his big bulldog head through the plastic window on the car. If a dog could think, Jack was probably thinking, *There, that's better. Now I have some air, and besides, I can see better.*

This time Jack didn't go along, and in a short while the rest of the family arrived at the meeting place in Buena Vista. In those days many evangelistic meetings were held in a big tent with sawdust on the floor, but this time the meetings were held in the Buena Vista Seventh-day Adventist Church. The children ran to the front to sit down, and Mother and Daddy Doss went up to the front, too, so that they could keep an eye on the children.

Soon the meeting started. There was congregational singing, special music, an enthusiastic welcome by Elder Coon's associate, and then the sermon by Elder Coon himself.

"We're so happy to have you folks here tonight," Elder Coon said to the Dosses at the close of the meeting. "We hope you plan to be here tomorrow morning."

"Well, I doubt it," replied Daddy Doss. "You see, we live in Lynchburg, and that is quite a distance to come."

"Oh, that can be taken care of very easily. Mrs. Coon and I would be happy to have you stay with us tonight." They could see he meant what he said, but they didn't want to impose.

"That would be too much to impose on you like that. We'd better not," said Mother Doss.

"It wouldn't be imposing at all, and we'd be so glad to have you." Mrs. Coon had come to where they were standing and added her request to her husband's.

So the Dosses went home with the Coons. By the time they arrived there, it was getting late, and the children were tired. But Desmond did remember one thing. The Coons had a big dormer window, the kind with one big window in the center, and one on each side that slanted toward the house. It made a space in front of the windows that had been filled in with a window seat. It was there Mrs. Coon made up a bed for Desmond. As he snuggled down into the blankets, he turned toward the window, and saw a sight he never forgot. Through all three of the windows he could see the stars shining down at him.

Next morning they got up and ate a hearty breakfast and then went back to the church for Sabbath School and the morning church service.

After dinner, Daddy Doss thought perhaps they should go home. But Mother Doss and the three children wanted to stay. They really enjoyed hearing Elder Coon speak. So Daddy gave in, and they stayed.

Elder Coon was an interesting person, filled with vim and vigor, as well as being a good speaker, and Daddy always did say he was the best preacher he ever knew. He always wore a tuxedo-type suit with long tails and a crisp white shirt with the tips of the collar turned down.

If people had eaten too much or the room was warm and people were inclined to sleep, he would hit the pulpit with a loud bang as he preached and ask, "Isn't that so, brethren?" Any sleepers would wake with a start!

After that meeting, Daddy thought they really should be going home. After all, at sunset the Sabbath would be over, and they always went to town on Saturday night and stocked up on groceries for the next week.

"Do they have anything in Lynchburg that you can't get right here in Buena Vista?" asked Elder Coon. The Dosses had to agree that they could get what they needed in Buena Vista. So, again, they decided to stay. After going to the store and buying groceries, they still arrived back at the church in time for the evening meeting.

Elder Coon's topic that night was the mark of the beast from the book of Revelation in the Bible. He explained that no one has the mark of the beast right now, but when Sunday laws are passed shortly before Jesus' second coming and people are convinced that they must choose to keep God's seventh-day Sabbath or man's first-day Sunday, then those who choose Sunday will receive the mark of the beast.

Then Elder Coon reminded people it was dangerous to put off a decision to do what God has asked us to do. His colorful remark was, "Anyone who knows what is right to do and does not do it is a spaghetti-back."

Thomas Doss had not thought of it just exactly like that before, and it gave him something to ponder as he drove back home that night.

Later he said to Bertha, "You know, I really feel that I should, and I really want to keep God's Sabbath, but if I did we would starve. It is hard to get work if you don't work on Saturdays."

Bertha's answer was, "Well, we can all starve together." She had been through hard times and had learned to depend on a loving God.

Thomas was happy for his wife's attitude. Shortly after the meetings in Buena Vista, Elder Clinton Coon, president of the Virginia Conference and the brother of Lester Coon, came to Lynchburg to hold a series of evangelistic meetings. Thomas and Bertha Doss and their children attended faithfully. More and more Thomas desired to become a Seventh-day Adventist church member, but before that time, he had a battle to fight with Mr. Nicotine.

When Mother Doss had worship with the three children every evening, each one always included in his or her prayer, "Dear Jesus, please help Daddy to stop smoking." The one being prayed for was usually in the dining room sitting in his old easy chair and reading the paper, holding it up in front of his face. But he was aware of the prayers.

One night just after worship with the usual prayers including the prayer for Daddy and his smoking habit, Mother Doss asked quietly, "Have you noticed that Daddy hasn't been smoking lately?"

"Really?"

"Yes, he hasn't smoked a cigarette for over three weeks now."

"Mom, that's wonderful. We didn't notice it," the three children chorused. Then they ran to where Daddy was sitting and let him know how glad they were that he wasn't smoking anymore. Daddy didn't say very much, but he was happy they noticed.

At the close of the series of meetings, Elder Clinton Coon baptized Daddy.

Just after Daddy Doss was baptized, he started out again to look for work. He was a carpenter and could get some part-time jobs at times, but nothing permanent. Again he went to see John Hancock, a building contractor. At times he could get a day or two of work there.

Thomas found John Hancock in his office. "Do you happen to have any work I could do?" he asked.

"Tom, I do have a small job you can do. Here is what I need to have done." And John explained what he could do.

The day happened to be Friday, and the job took more time than either Thomas or John thought it would. In the late afternoon John came around to see how the job was coming and saw that it needed more work to finish it up.

"Thomas, you are doing a good job, but you won't finish that tonight. Come in tomorrow and finish it," John suggested.

"I'm sorry, John, but tomorrow is my Sabbath—no, God's Sabbath— and I can't work then," said Thomas.

"Well, then come in and get your money tomorrow," was John's further suggestion.

"Sorry, John, I can't do that either. But I'll come in Monday for my pay," said Thomas.

"OK, Tom." And Mr. Doss left for home to spend Friday evening and Sabbath with his family, going to Sabbath School and church.

When Thomas went in Monday morning to pick up his pay, he met John.

"Tom, that job still isn't finished. Want to finish it?" asked John.

"Sure, I'll be glad to," answered Tom, and he got out the tools that he needed and soon finished the job.

John Hancock came to Thomas just as he was finishing, and said, "Tom, I have another job you can do if you are interested." Of course, Tom was, and he worked on that job for the rest of the day. From then on Thomas always had work to do, and he knew it was because he was faithfully doing, with God's help, what he had known was right for a long time.

Now that Father and Mother were both working, things were looking up for the finances of the Doss family.

MEMORIES—IV

Desmond had finished his grade school education, but book learning came hard for him, so he decided to get a job. He found work at the Lynchburg Lumber Company—at eight cents per hour. It was hard work, too. He helped unload car loads of lumber, kept wood scraps and shavings near the furnace where the fires were kindled to provide steam to run the machinery, and unloaded one- and two-hundred pound bags of fertilizer. For a teenager who weighed only 125 pounds, it was hard work. He worked fifty hours per week, too.

By the time he arrived home at night, he was so tired he could hardly eat. Then he would sit on the couch and go right off to sleep. Mother Doss would wake him up so he could go to bed.

Later his pay was raised to ten cents per hour. He would pay his tithe, following the good example of his mother, and put fifty cents away for savings as she suggested. Then he would give his mother three dollars to help her pay the grocery bill. That left one dollar for clothes and anything else he wanted or needed. He could still remember how upset he was when the lumber company started to take out five cents per paycheck for Social Security.

His mother liked to encourage her children, and there was one way she encouraged Desmond. He needed some new clothes to replace some badly worn ones. When a relative or friend dropped in, Mother would call their attention to Desmond's new shoes or a new pair of pants, perhaps, and tell them how Desmond was buying his own clothes now. She never did tell them how she helped him buy the clothes with money she earned.

★ ★ ★ ★ ★

Then Desmond remembered another experience he had that made him realize that he needed to watch his example.

One day he was walking over to Aunt Ella's to cut the lawn for her. As he came near the trestle that went over the street, he noticed a man up on the trestle whom he knew was an alcoholic. He remembered what his mother had told him about those who drink: "Beware of people who drink. You can't trust them."

This alcoholic saw him and hurried down to where he was. "Buddy, do you have a match? I need one," he said.

35

Desmond answered, "I'm sorry, but I don't smoke."

"I know you don't," the man said.

Desmond mentioned he was going over to his aunt's house to do some work.

The man surprised Desmond by saying, "I know where she lives. I also know where you live and that you are a seven-day boy and where you go to church and where you work, and I know you don't fight."

The man seemed to know more about Desmond than he knew about himself. It made Desmond think that if this man, an alcoholic whom he had never seen sober, was watching him and knew what his habits were, then how many others were watching him even more closely? He really needed to be careful of his example as a Seventh-day Adventist Christian, and not be a stumbling block to others.

★ ★ ★ ★ ★

The big troop ship had sailed out of Hawaii several days before. *We really should be getting someplace soon,* Desmond thought. He didn't know whether he would be happy to get off the rolling ship or whether he would just as soon stay on. What would combat be like?

As he prayed that night, he asked God to go with him and keep him safe as he went into battle. "And be with the folks and Dorothy," he finished.

CHAPTER FIVE

MEMORIES—V

It had been several days since the troop ship left Hawaii. Desmond knew they had been doing a certain amount of zigzagging as a safety measure. Also they were keeping their eyes open for Japanese ships, submarines, or aircraft. Once Desmond had been below in his bunk when he heard sort of a ripping sound under the ship and wondered what it was. He went up on deck to ask.

"Didn't you see that?" the other soldiers asked. "A torpedo was coming right toward the ship, and then it suddenly changed direction and went under the ship." Desmond felt that angels had guided the torpedo away from the ship, but it had come close enough to barely scrape the bottom. He said a prayer of thanksgiving to God.

That night on deck he sat down on his box. The weather was pleasant out there on the Pacific, and he was enjoying the memories.

★ ★ ★ ★ ★

Grandma raised Maltese cats; she thought they were the best cats alive. But the neighborhood tomcats would often come to socialize with her cats, resulting in crossbred kittens.

Dad would shoot the tomcats from his window next door whenever he could. Grandma was afraid Dad might kill one of her cats, but they seemed to have a sixth sense of danger when the window flew up, and they would run under the house.

"Desmond," said Grandma one day, "there are seven of these crossbred kittens I want to get rid of. If you will take them to the creek and drown them, I'll pay you a penny apiece." He started out toward the creek with the kittens in a paper sack, and dumped the whole sack upside down into the water. When he saw the little kittens in the water, he tried to rescue them, but they drowned anyway. He couldn't remember now whether he ever received the seven cents, but from that time on he would never drown a cat no matter how much money he was offered.

Thinking of animals reminded him of how he became a vegetarian.

Grandma also raised chickens, and every once in a while she would go to the chicken yard, catch a chicken, wring its neck, clean it, and cook it for dinner. Desmond liked to eat chicken, too. But one day . . .

"Desmond, how about you killing a chicken for dinner today?" Grandma said.

"Me, Grandma? Oh, I don't want to kill a chicken." Desmond sort of shivered as he said it.

"Well, you like to eat them, don't you? If you can eat them, you can kill them," said Grandma.

He thought about how those poor chickens would flop around with their heads off just so that he could enjoy eating them.

"Grandma, I won't eat them anymore," he said, and he didn't.

Sometime later Desmond became acquainted with a young man who worked at the Kennedy slaughterhouse in Lynchburg.

"Leroy, I sure would like to visit that slaughterhouse some day," said Desmond.

"Well, why don't you? Come tomorrow afternoon. I don't work then, and I could show you through," invited Leroy.

Desmond arrived as planned. He said later that he was absolutely shocked at what he saw. A number of the cows were skin and bones and looked sick. One even had a broken leg but was pushed along with the others and slaughtered. The pigs were treated even worse. He felt sorry for the poor animals.

"They cut the meat off the bones of the cows, even when they are sick. Oh, if they have sores, they cut the sores out. Then they grind up all this meat, and make hamburger out of it," explained Leroy.

Desmond loved hamburger. He thought of how his mother would make patties and then cover them with gravy. Mmmmm! But after that trip to the slaughterhouse, he lost all appetite for hamburger. He chose to become a vegetarian.

* * * * *

Then Desmond recalled another time when he knew God had protected him.

"My ball! Uncle Desmond, my ball! See it? Please get it for me." Five-year-old Ronnie looked pleadingly at his uncle.

Ronnie and his family were having an outing on the shores of the Atlantic Ocean, and Ronnie was playing with his new red, yellow, and white beach ball near the shore. Somehow it had gotten away from him and seemed to be drifting out to sea.

Eighteen-year-old Uncle Desmond was not a very good swimmer, but he could swim some, and the ball wasn't far out in the ocean, so he jumped in and started to swim after the big beach ball. He swam very hard, but somehow that pesky beach ball stayed ahead of him. He wasn't making much progress in catching it.

When he stopped to tread water for a few moments, he looked around and was really frightened by what he saw. He was out much farther than he thought he was. Suddenly it dawned on him that the tide was going out. That was the reason the ball was keeping ahead of him. That was the reason he had gone so far in such a short time.

"Now what will I do?" he said to himself. He realized that swimming back against the tide would be impossible. Also he was getting very tired! His only hope was to catch that ball and use it as a sort of life preserver to hold him up. But he couldn't catch it!

Desmond was used to praying about things, but he had never been in this kind of trouble before. "Lord, help me!" he prayed.

He looked around. There was the ball, floating a little farther away. Then he noticed something else he hadn't seen before—a boat. It was just a small fishing boat with a motor on it. Two men seemed to be pulling in their fishing gear and preparing to go out farther into the ocean. The waves weren't high, but they were high enough that sometimes he could see the boat and sometimes not. He knew the fishermen could not always see him even if they were looking in his direction.

"Lord, help them to see me," he prayed.

"Help!" he yelled. But with their motor running, the men did not hear him or pay any attention to him. They started to head out farther into the ocean, but then they seemed to see the big beach ball and started to steer the boat toward it. They picked the ball out of the water.

"Hey, there is a man here, too," one said. Soon the boat was beside Desmond.

"Here, let me help you in. It's sure a good thing we saw you. You needed help." Desmond couldn't agree with them more. He knew Jesus helped them to see him.

Not much was said as they headed for shore. The motor was making too much noise. Soon they were close to the shore. "Can you make it from here?" one of the men asked.

"Yes, this will be fine. And thank you so much," said Desmond, as he took his beach ball and jumped over the side into shallow water. He climbed out of the water and then looked around to wave another time to the men, as a "thank you" gesture.

There were no men! No boat! Not even a ripple on the water! Were those two men angels sent in answer to his prayer?

As Desmond thought about this experience again, he really believed they were.

★ ★ ★ ★ ★

Desmond's memories and the time he had to think about them were both coming to an end. He imagined the ship must be getting to some destination soon, although he still didn't know what that destination was. His memories now were of more recent happenings.

After working for the Lynchburg Lumber Company for a year, he worked for the city for a while. He remembered how he and the other workers had built a fire on a very cold day, but it didn't help because of the extreme cold. That day his pick had slipped off the side of the icy ditch where they were working and hit Desmond's foot. He didn't realize until he got home that the pick had gone through his shoe and cut into his foot. His foot was so numb it didn't even hurt and so cold it didn't even bleed!

The last job he had before he was drafted into the army was at the shipyard in Newport News, Virginia. Even before World War II started, the shipyard was readying ships to be used in the military—revamping and rebuilding. Some of the ships had been luxury liners, and Desmond remembered how all of the luxuries were torn out, such as rugs and room furnishings, leaving bare floors and bare staterooms. These were filled with canvas bunks for the men, providing a very limited space for each soldier.

He also thought about the more famous ships he had seen and worked on at the shipyard. He had worked twice on the America, the country's largest luxury ship. The first time they eliminated all of the luxury. Two months later it came in again for more alterations. This time they closed in the decks so that they could put in more bunks for the military men to sleep on.

From time to time he saw the USS *Hornet* being changed into an aircraft carrier. Desmond was living with Elder Harry Gray at the time, and two of his sons were electricians on the *Hornet*. Desmond saw the *Hornet* every day as he went to work on the *Indiana,* the ship he was working on at the time.

"I'd like to see that big boat you are working on," he said to Jimmy Gray one day.

"Come ahead. I'll show you around," answered Jimmy.

But Desmond didn't think it would be quite right to take off time from his work to see the other ship, so he never did. But later he wished he had.

When he saw the *Hornet* being worked on, he did not know that it would carry the planes that would bomb Tokyo, Japan, in 1943. The bombers were a daring group led by Jimmy Doolittle. Later Doolittle was given the Congressional Medal of Honor for his leadership and heroism at that time. Because Doss and Doolittle were close together in the alphabet, Desmond often ate with Jimmy Doolittle at certain military functions.

★ ★ ★ ★ ★

By this time Desmond Doss had been in the army for approximately two and a half years. It was the summer of 1944, and he was to take part in overseas fighting for the first time.

The next section of this book will be about his experiences in the Army of the United States of America.

CHAPTER SIX

WAR!

"Desmond, wouldn't you like to go to New York this weekend?" asked his friend, Robert Taylor.

"Why? What's up?" Desmond answered his friend's question with a question.

"I haven't seen my folks for a long time, and I don't think my old car would make the trip. You have a pretty good car. I'd pay for the gas and a little extra besides. How about it?" said Robert.

"OK. When do we leave?" asked Desmond.

"Friday, and come back Sunday," answered Robert.

At this time the United States government was drafting young men to serve for one year in the military. Robert was one of these draftees, and he had only one more month of his year to serve.

The boys had to wait until after work on Friday, so they got a late start for the three-hundred-mile trip to New York. At one place they were on a two-lane road, and it was so dark Desmond couldn't see the road.

"Hey," he said to Robert, "see that big limousine up ahead? I'm going to follow it."

The limousine was well lit up and was going pretty fast. Desmond managed to keep up with it. But on Sunday when they drove back home, he saw that the road they had driven on was actually a narrow mountain road with an even narrower shoulder. He thanked the Lord they had gotten over that stretch without dropping off the side of the mountain. Had that happened, they surely would have been killed.

WAR!

Desmond and Robert were getting ready to leave the Taylor home on Sunday.

"Thanks so much for the good time, Mom and Dad," said Robert as they were packing things into the car. "And the delicious food," he added.

"Yes, it's been so nice to be here," chimed in Desmond. "Thanks a lot."

They were soon driving the highway that Sunday, enjoying the warmth of the car on a cold December day. The radio was on. Suddenly the musical program on the radio stopped. For a second there was silence. Then—"Japan has bombed Pearl Harbor in Hawaii. America is at war! Any military personnel not at your camp are to report there immediately. I repeat, America is at war with Japan."

Robert and Desmond looked at each other, disbelief written all over their faces. The announcement began to sink in.

"I guess that is the end of my plans for one more month of military service," Robert remarked rather shakily. "I'll probably be in for the duration. Wonder how long it will last?"

"Who knows? I will probably be joining you in the military soon," said Desmond. He had never been called up for the one-year draft because he had quite a high number and because he was working in the shipyard, which was considered an essential industry to the government's military plans.

As the two boys drove on down the road that afternoon of December 7, 1941, their thoughts were on the future and what it would hold for them.

Three times that day before they got home, they were stopped by the police. Because Robert was in uniform, the police wanted to know where the two boys were going. After Robert explained to them that they had been in New York and were heading back to his camp, they waved them on.

As they drove, Desmond was thinking of the day when he went to the draft board to register as was required of all males eighteen years old. Elder Wood, the minister of his church, went with him. They waited in the hall until a draft board officer called them in.

Four or five officers were in the room. After they had taken his name and address, they were ready to give him a classification.

"I'd like to register as a noncombatant," Desmond told them.

"Son, there isn't any such thing in the army," an officer answered.

"You see, Sir," Desmond even remembered to address the officer as sir, "I belong to the Seventh-day Adventist Church, and we can't do regular duties on Saturday, the Sabbath. We can take care of sick or hurt people on Sabbath like Jesus did."

"What does that have to do with being a noncombatant?" asked another officer.

"Well, we believe we need to keep all of the Ten Commandments. One of them is 'Thou shalt not kill.' So we don't believe in using a gun," answered Desmond. Elder Wood nodded his head in agreement and seemed to be pleased with Desmond's answers.

The draft board officer looked puzzled. "What if everyone felt that way, young man? How could we ever fight a war?"

"If they all felt that way, there would be no wars," Desmond replied. "But, Sir, soldiers are going to get hurt, and I would like to help take care of them."

"OK, Doss, but you will need to register as a conscientious objector then," proposed still another officer.

"But, Sir, I'm not a conscientious objector." Desmond recalled what he knew of conscientious objectors. They demonstrated against the government, and they wouldn't salute the flag, wear a military uniform, or do anything to help the war effort. He didn't want to be lumped with them.

"Well, you see, Son, you tell me you want to keep the Sabbath on Saturday and that you won't carry a gun. If you went into the army with a 1A classification and wanted to keep your Sabbath or not carry a gun, I can assure you, you would soon be court-martialed. But if you have the 1AO classification—the O stands for conscientious objector—even the army can't court-martial you. So, you see, that would be best for you," explained the officer. "Being a conscientious objector doesn't mean you won't serve your country. It only means you go into the army with religious scruples or reservations."

Desmond looked at Elder Wood, and Elder Wood looked at Desmond.

"Desmond, I think it would be best for you to take that classification as he suggests. There isn't much else you can do," said Elder Wood.

Desmond remembered this as he drove his car home that Sunday afternoon. What would the future hold for him? He had no doubt that he would soon be called up for military service.

He was right. Soon his "greetings" came in the mail, and on April 1, 1942, Desmond was inducted into the United States Army. It was not an April Fools' Day joke, either.

CHAPTER SEVEN

DOROTHY

Let's go back to 1920. Fred and Elsie Schutte were living in Colorado at the time. Fred had been gassed during World War I and was on permanent disability. Elsie was pregnant with their first child and was very happy about it.

But she was not feeling very well, so Fred hired a lady in the community to give Elsie some help with her housekeeping and cooking duties. Betty (we will call her that) was a Seventh-day Adventist, and she loved to read her Bible and tell others about it whenever she had the opportunity. It wasn't long until she was telling Elsie things about the Bible that Elsie had never heard before. Betty carefully explained the Sabbath, what happens to people when they die, Jesus' second coming in the clouds of heaven, and other Bible truths.

"That surely does sound reasonable, even though I have never heard anything like it before," Elsie told Betty one day. Then Elsie started to study on her own with the Bible Betty gave her.

"I really believe this is the truth from the Bible," Elsie told her friend, Betty, one day—for these two ladies had become good friends as they studied the Bible together. "I'd really like to join your church, but how can I? My husband was brought up a Catholic, and he wants me to go to that church."

"I'm sorry about that, Elsie," Betty remarked, "but I'll tell you what. You keep studying your Bible, and things will work out eventually, I'm sure."

Shortly after that Fred and Elsie decided to go back to live in Richmond, Virginia, where their people lived. On the way to Virginia, it became

DESMOND DOSS

necessary for them to stop in Philadelphia, Pennsylvania, for the birth of their baby daughter, whom they named Dorothy Pauline.

As Dorothy told Desmond much later, the Schutte home was not a happy home. In the first place, Fred was not happy because Elsie was interested in a different religion from the one he was raised in, even though he seldom attended church. He didn't even want her to read the Bible that had become so precious to her.

"I don't want you reading that old book all the time," he angrily said to her one day. So saying, he grabbed the Bible out of her hands and threw it into the kitchen stove.

This was a number of years after Dorothy was born. Six other children had joined the family by this time. Their father had acquired the habit of drinking liquor and had become an alcoholic. Drink always brought out the worst in him, and he was many times abusive to his wife and children.

He would often come home from the corner store where he bought liquor and drank with his friends and begin beating his children. One day Dorothy protested with a sob, "Daddy, why did you beat me? I didn't do anything wrong."

"That is to make up for the times you have done bad things and didn't get beaten," he answered unfeelingly.

It seemed he liked to "take it out" on the two older children especially, so Dorothy and Thomas learned to hide when they saw their father coming home. When Dorothy was fifteen, her father died—probably as a result of his general health and his drinking. She said later that it was like hell followed by heaven in the Schutte home. After his death, Mother Schutte and the children started going to church each Sabbath; soon she and the older children were baptized into the Seventh-day Adventist Church. Mother Schutte made arrangements for the children to attend the church school, which was in a room at the back of the church.

But Dorothy had finished the eighth grade by now and was ready to attend Shenandoah Valley Academy, a high school–level boarding school where the students could learn about the Bible as well as other subjects. Dorothy wanted to attend this Seventh-day Adventist academy, so she talked it over with her mother.

"Mother, I would really like to go to school there. I would learn so much about the Bible, and it would also be fun to live in the dormitory with the other girls," said Dorothy.

"But Dorothy, can we afford it? It would be kind of expensive," observed Mother.

"I can work at the academy, you know. There are a lot of things a student can do there, like helping in the kitchen with meals and dish washing—I've done enough of that so I know how—working in the laundry or on the grounds cutting lawns or working in the offices if you can do that kind of work. There are also a few industries so students can earn money there. I'd work every minute they would let me, and I'm sure I could earn much of my way."

"All right, Dorothy, see what you can find out about it. Write to the school for information and get an application blank," suggested Mother.

That is the way Dorothy found her way to Shenandoah Valley Academy, and she soon learned to love it there.

Another thing students could do to help pay their school bill was to sell religious magazines and books during the summer months. One day at the academy, Dorothy was talking to her roommate. "Mary, why don't we sell magazines this summer? It would give us some money for our school bill next year," suggested Dorothy.

"Why don't we? If you will go along with me, I'm willing to try. Just think, we might be able to make enough for our whole school bill next year," replied Mary.

The girls were probably a little more enthusiastic than the situation called for, but what could anyone accomplish if it weren't for dreams? So with the help and encouragement of the leader for such activities, they made arrangements to sell magazines. They were assigned to go to Lynchburg, Virginia.

It was at church in Lynchburg that Desmond first met Dorothy.

At this time Desmond was working for the city and living at home. Whoever got home from work first on Friday afternoon was the one who worked on cooking dinner for Sabbath. By this time Audrey was married, and Harold wasn't really interested in cooking, so most of the cooking was done by Mother Doss and Desmond.

One Friday Desmond arrived home first, so he started to cook. There always had to be a pot of navy beans, so he dumped some beans into the big pan, covered them with water, and set them on the stove to cook.

Then he cut up some vegetables and made a delicious vegetable stew. By the time he finished cooking the beans and stew, he was feeling pretty good about his Sabbath dinner.

"Mother, do you suppose we could invite Dorothy and Mary—you know, those two girls who are selling magazines in Lynchburg this summer—to come home and eat dinner with us tomorrow? It would be fun," Desmond suggested later that evening.

Hospitable Mrs. Doss said, "Yes, of course, Desmond."

The next day, when Desmond saw the girls at church, he asked, "Dorothy, could you and Mary come home and eat dinner at our house today?"

The girls looked at each other, and they both said "Yes" together. Desmond didn't realize that these girls weren't doing very well at selling magazines and that their food supply wasn't very adequate. They were hungry! In fact, they could remember one day when they didn't have any food or any money to buy any food.

One man bought a magazine from them for a dime when they told him they were hungry. With the dime they bought a loaf of day-old bread and a fourth of a pound of butter—and ate it all at one sitting! So that day Dorothy and Mary were very happy to be going to the Dosses for dinner.

Desmond unobtrusively took his mother aside when they arrived home and told her, "Mom, entertain the girls a little, will you. I can heat up the dinner."

"All right, Desmond, if that's what you want," said Mother.

So Desmond set the beans and stew on the stove and turned the burners up high to get them heated faster. Then he got out some crackers, sliced the bread, and got some other things ready to put on the table.

What was that smell? Oh, those beans! Desmond grabbed them off the stove. They had boiled dry, and the smell indicated that they were burning. He dumped them into another pan, being careful to leave the burned ones on the bottom of the pan. Then he put more water on the beans and set them back on the stove, but turned the heat down. He scraped the burned ones into a bowl—he could eat those later.

Just as he thought he had everything under control, the burned smell came to his nostrils again. What next? The stew! He grabbed it off the stove and went through the same process with it. It was too late to make anything else, and besides you didn't waste things in the Doss household.

DOROTHY

He tasted the stew. It did taste slightly scorched, but he felt it was edible. So he called the others to dinner.

One time, much later, Desmond reminded Dorothy of that dinner and the burned beans and stew. They had a good laugh over it. Dorothy said, "We were so hungry we didn't even know the beans were scorched."

Eventually Dorothy and Mary went back to their beloved Shenandoah Valley Academy, and Desmond was busy with other things—such as working. Three or four years went by, and he was working in the shipyard at Newport News.

One day at church he met Mrs. Hildebrandt. He remembered her as the one who was in charge of the girls when they were selling magazines.

"Mrs. Hildebrandt, do you happen to know where Dorothy Schutte is now? I haven't kept up with her and don't know where she is," Desmond asked.

"Why yes, Desmond," she answered. "She graduated from Shenandoah Valley Academy, and she is now attending Washington Missionary College. That is actually in Takoma Park, a Washington, D.C., suburb. The General Conference of Seventh-day Adventists, the Review and Herald Publishing Company, and the Washington Sanitarium and Hospital are all in the same area."

That was all Desmond needed to know. The next weekend, he was in the Washington, D.C., area—hoping he could see Dorothy.

There were three Adventist churches in the area—the big Sligo church, the hospital church, and the college church at Washington Missionary College. He decided that probably Dorothy would be at the college church, so he went there. He stayed in front of the church for a few minutes to see if he could see Dorothy come in with the other students, but no Dorothy. He decided to slip in and worship with that group anyway. Perhaps he could find Dorothy later. He sat down near the back and immediately noticed Dorothy in the seat just ahead of him.

He tapped her on the shoulder. She looked around and got a very surprised look on her face. He wanted to whisper to her then, but she, knowing the rules, said, "Shhh. I'll talk to you later."

It is doubtful whether Desmond heard much of what the preacher said that day. After church, he did get a chance to talk to Dorothy.

"It is good to see you, Dorothy. It's been a long time since I last saw you. I guess it was when we were both in Lynchburg."

"Desmond, it's nice to see you, too. Yes, it was at Lynchburg. Seems like a long time ago," remarked Dorothy.

"Can't we eat dinner together somewhere?" Desmond had found Dorothy, and he wasn't about to let her get away so quickly.

"The Millers—they are some people in the church here—asked me to eat dinner with them, so I don't know . . ." her voice trailed off.

Just then the Millers came to where he and Dorothy were standing to pick up Dorothy and take her home to dinner.

Desmond didn't lose any time in explaining to them, "I came to see Dorothy today. She didn't know I was coming. But I'd like to take her out to dinner."

"Why, of course, Dorothy," said Mrs. Miller. "You go ahead. You can come over to our place another day." So the Millers got in their car and left, leaving Desmond and Dorothy alone.

"Now, Dorothy, you know more about this place than I do. Where is a good place to eat?" asked Desmond.

"Well, there are two places. One is the college cafeteria. The other is the dining room at the hospital," answered Dorothy.

"Where would you rather go?" he asked.

"I usually go to the college cafeteria," she answered.

Thinking of the rules of the college that boyfriends shouldn't be eating with girlfriends, a rule that we would consider quite out of date now, Dorothy hoped that anyone who knew her would think Desmond was her cousin or something. But, after all, he wasn't her boyfriend, she told herself. Just an acquaintance.

So Desmond and Dorothy ate dinner together at the college cafeteria. Later they found a place where they could visit.

"What are you taking in college, Dorothy?" Desmond asked her.

"Pre-nursing right now. I hope to get into nursing next year. What are you doing?" she asked.

"Working in the shipyard at Newport News, Virginia. I'm a joiner—like a carpenter, only we mostly work on the inside of those big ships. We can work on rainy days that way," he answered.

Questions flew back and forth, and the young couple enjoyed the afternoon together. Desmond knew he must soon leave, as he had a two-hundred-mile trip home that night.

"You don't mind if I come to see you again, do you?"

Desmond watched Dorothy closely as she answered, with a smile on her face, "Come ahead if you want to. I've enjoyed today."

From then on, for Desmond, it was a trip one weekend to see his parents at Lynchburg and the next weekend to see Dorothy at Washington Missionary College. Then he would repeat the weekends. He found himself especially enjoying the weekends with Dorothy.

Later, when Desmond and Dorothy had become much better friends, they were double-dating with another couple. "Why don't you drive my car this time and let Dorothy and me sit in the back for a change?" suggested Desmond to his friend.

"OK with me," he said. "I don't think I can hurt your old car," he joked.

Now Desmond really didn't plan for things to happen as they did. But here was Dorothy right beside him, and so close!

He bent over and kissed her on the cheek. He surely didn't expect what happened next. She turned around and almost slapped his face!

"Desmond, NO! What do you mean by kissing me? That's the first time I have ever let a boy kiss me. But I didn't let you. You did it without asking." Desmond could tell she was really angry with him.

"I was afraid if I asked you," he said meekly, "you wouldn't let me. But Dorothy, I kissed you because I really do love you. I wouldn't be driving four hundred miles a weekend to see you if I weren't interested in you, would I?"

"No, I guess you wouldn't," Dorothy answered, and there was a look of wonder and happiness on her face. From then on things went a lot more smoothly, and Desmond and Dorothy loved being together whenever they could.

So it was only natural that when Desmond and Robert Taylor were driving back to Newport News from New York that night of December 7, 1941, Desmond would want to stop for a few minutes to talk to Dorothy about the war.

While Robert wandered around in the area, Desmond went to the home where Dorothy was staying and working for her room and board while she was in college. She was just beginning to study for her next day's classes when the lady for whom she was working came to her door and told her she had a visitor. The lady purposely didn't tell her who it was, and Dorothy was puzzled. She knew Desmond wasn't planning to see her that weekend.

She squealed with delight when she saw Desmond. But she soon realized he was in a very serious frame of mind.

"Dorothy, have you heard the news?" asked Desmond.

"What news?" she asked, with a little twinge of fear showing in her eyes.

"Japan has bombed Pearl Harbor, and America and Japan are at war," he answered.

"No, I hadn't heard that. Desmond, does that mean you will have to go to war?" she asked again.

"I suppose so," he answered. "I'm sure in line for the draft."

They talked a few minutes longer, and then Desmond knew he must leave as he still had a long trip home. That time when he took Dorothy in his arms and gave her a goodbye kiss, there was no protest.

CHAPTER EIGHT

"YOU'RE IN THE ARMY NOW"

Desmond realized that the time was nearing when he would actually be in the army, but he still worked at the shipyard waiting for his draft notice. "Desmond, do you have any idea when you will be leaving for the service?" asked his boss at the shipyard one day.

"I don't actually know when," answered Desmond, "but it has to be soon judging by the numbers they are calling now. They are very near my number."

"You know, you are working in an essential industry, and we could try to get you on the deferred list," suggested the boss. "I think we could do it. So many of our workers are going into the army that we're shorthanded now."

"Well, I don't think I should try to be deferred. My health is good; I don't have any worries on that score. And I don't believe I'm any better than the other fellows who are going in at twenty-one dollars a month. Thanks anyway, but I think I should go," answered Desmond.

"Suit yourself. I thought I would offer you the chance anyway." And the boss walked away to take care of other duties. Now that the service issue was definitely decided, Desmond felt there was one other thing that needed to be decided, too.

He was in Washington again, and he and Dorothy had spent a beautiful Sabbath together. On Sunday afternoon, after Dorothy had finished her work for the day at the home where she was working, Desmond picked her up for a ride down to the park before he had to start home.

"Have you heard anything more about when you will be going to the army?" Dorothy asked.

"Nothing definite yet. I told you the boss at the shipyard offered me a deferment, didn't I?" asked Desmond.

"Yes, you told me that, and I admire you for taking the attitude that you did, even though it would have been easier for you if you had stayed out of the army," remarked Dorothy.

Desmond parked the car near a pretty little creek where they had enjoyed some happy times together. Now he leaned closer to Dorothy, put his arm around her shoulders, and squeezed tightly as he asked, "Dorothy, I love you so much, and I would like for you to be my wife. Would you?"

"I love you, too, Desmond, and I'd like nothing better than to be your wife," was Dorothy's welcome reply. There were other words of endearment, and this time Dorothy had no objection to the kisses of the man who had won her heart. However, these were war years, and couples who wanted to get married had to remember this as they made plans for the future.

"We have some problems, Desmond," said Dorothy as they discussed the whole situation. "One of them is that I plan to be a nursing student in September, and the nursing school won't let me get married. Well, they can't really stop me, but if I get married, I can't go to nursing school. They feel it is better if students aren't married. And I really want to be a nurse."

"I know you do, sweetheart, and we aren't going to keep you from being a nurse. Another problem is that if I go in the army and am sent overseas, it would leave you alone. What if you had a baby?" asked Desmond.

"I've thought a lot about that, Desmond. When I have a baby, I want to be a full-time mother. But, if we had a baby, and you had to go overseas, it would leave me all alone, and I would have to work. Worse yet," Dorothy added with a catch in her voice, "what if we had a baby and you didn't come back? How could I raise a child by myself?"

As they discussed these things, they decided that as much as they loved each other and would like to get married, it would be best if they waited until after the war for the wedding. They knew that many other couples had come to the same conclusion. This was a part of war.

★ ★ ★ ★ ★

It was April 1, 1942, and the army was claiming its new recruits.

"Name?" questioned the admitting officer.

"Doss, Desmond T.," answered the new recruit.

"You are from here in Lynchburg, aren't you?" the officer said as he looked at Desmond's papers.

"Yes, Sir," said Desmond.

"OK, Doss. Go over there with that group of men. You will be shipping out to Camp Lee in a little while," he said.

Soon the new recruits were on the train. Desmond noticed that most of the fellows were just kids eighteen or nineteen years old. He was twenty-three. All seemed to be somewhat nervous. Desmond had a little more to think about than the others, he supposed. It happened to be Friday; the next day would be Sabbath. What would happen?

As he sat back and tried to relax, Desmond became aware of the awful smell of tobacco smoke and also whiskey and beer. The recruits were not actually sworn into the army as yet—that would come at Camp Lee. So they were doing a little last minute celebrating. Nearly every fellow on the troop train was drinking and smoking. And their cigarettes were actually big, black cigars. Many of them became so drunk they could hardly stand up.

By the time the train pulled into Camp Lee, Desmond felt as if he had been smoking, himself. He had a splitting headache.

"All out, fellows. Go over to that building," ordered the officer in charge.

Desmond jumped out, got in line, and after some time was at the table where a soldier was issuing uniforms and other gear.

"Let's see. You're Doss, eh? What are your sizes, Doss?" After Desmond told him, he brought out two uniforms, underclothes, shoes, socks, and a heavy coat, together with a duffel bag to put them all in.

"Change into your army clothes, Doss," he said, "and bring your civvies back over to that table; the guys there will help you send them back home. You won't need them in the army."

When Desmond had done all this, he felt like another person. Where did the other Desmond go?

After receiving their army clothing, the new recruits were directed to the various barracks where they would be sleeping for the next couple of nights that they would be at this center. Since this was an induction center, the fellows were not restricted as yet, so Desmond went into Petersburg for the Friday night meeting at the Seventh-day Adventist church. He would have liked to return the next morning for church services, but it didn't work out quite that way.

Sabbath morning, he awoke to hear the sergeant bark, "OK, guys, time to rise and shine. We've got work to do today. You're in the army now—you don't lie around all day Saturday like at home."

Desmond got up with the rest of the guys, dressed, and went to the mess hall for breakfast. He didn't know how the rest of the day would work out, but he did know he couldn't do certain activities on the Sabbath.

After breakfast, the sergeant announced, "OK, gang. Later on today we have inspection. That means we have to have these barracks clean—and I mean clean!" said the sergeant. "The floors have to be mopped, all of the cupboards dusted and the insides cleaned out, beds made perfectly—no wrinkles—and the outside around our barracks cleaned. Everything that doesn't grow has to be picked up. Oh, yes, don't forget the windows—they have to sparkle inside and out. Remember the ones who inspect wear white gloves, and woe to all of you if you leave any dust even on the tops of the cupboards. The mops, mop pails, and cleaning supplies are in this cupboard. Any questions, ask me. So get busy!"

This was Desmond's time to speak to the sergeant. "Sergeant, Sir," he said. "I'm a Seventh-day Adventist, and today is my Sabbath. I can't do that kind of work on Sabbath."

"You're what? What on earth is a Seventh-day Adventist, and why can't you help with the cleaning, mama's boy?" The sergeant spit out the words.

"I'm not afraid to clean. But I can't do it on my Sabbath. You see, I am a CO—conscientious objector."

"Well, what do you know? We have a CO," the sergeant said sarcastically. "Buddy, you need to know that I have no use for guys like you. Now, get to work."

"I'm sorry, Sir, but I can't," said Desmond. "I'll work tomorrow, twice as hard. I promise."

"We need you today, not tomorrow. If you won't work, get out of here before I throw you out! I don't want you in my sight."

"YOU'RE IN THE ARMY NOW"

So Desmond went out and sat on the barracks steps. He pulled his little Bible from his pocket and started to read. The last few minutes had been like a nightmare, and he needed some encouragement from his Bible.

"Well, what do we have here?" an officer was walking by and saw Desmond sitting on the steps, reading his Bible. "You aren't supposed to be outside the barracks right now. Get back inside and go to work."

Desmond tried to explain, but the officer wouldn't listen. He only repeated, "Get back inside."

So, with a sigh, Desmond got up and went back in the door of the barracks. The sergeant spotted him. "I thought I told you to get outside!" he exclaimed.

"I was," said Desmond, "but an officer told me to come back in."

"What a pretty kettle of fish this is! OK, Doss, get over in that corner out of the way so the other guys won't trip over you," he said sarcastically.

So Desmond went and sat in the corner, while every soldier who got near enough "cussed him out."

Next morning the recruits were told to get their things together and be out by the tracks by 10:00 A.M. They were going to Fort Jackson in South Carolina for basic training.

CHAPTER NINE

BASIC TRAINING

"Hop on that train, you army guys. Might as well make yourselves comfortable because it will be a long trip. Besides, once you arrive, you won't have time to be comfortable," the army officer pointed out.

It was a beautiful ride down through southern Virginia and on through North Carolina into South Carolina to Fort Jackson near Columbia. The men were directed to leave the train and get into the army vehicles that were on hand to pick them up and take them to Fort Jackson.

On arrival at the camp, they were directed to tables where they were given information and assignments. When it was his turn, Desmond approached the table and gave the officer a rather awkward salute because he hadn't learned the technique yet. The officer returned the salute with a grin.

Then he took Desmond's papers, looked them over, and said, "Doss, your army number is 33158036. Your medical records number is C6067288. Here is a card with the numbers on it, but I'd suggest you learn them. You'll use them a lot. We're assigning you to Company M. That soldier at the door will direct you."

"Where is Company M?" Desmond asked the soldier.

The soldier gave him directions but then said, "Wait. They want everyone to wait here until you get some more instructions."

The instructors read the Article of War to the men and told them not to go AWOL—absent without leave—and other things. Then they said, "You are quarantined for the next two weeks. You do not leave Fort Jackson during that time." Then they were dismissed.

BASIC TRAINING

Desmond found Company M and got his gear neatly stowed away at the end of his bunk. It was the beginning of the week, and Desmond decided he should not wait until Friday afternoon to ask about the Sabbath. He wanted to be sure he wasn't assigned to a work detail for that day. But also he wanted to go to church. He wondered how that would work out when he heard about the quarantine. Before he left his bunk area he prayed a little prayer, asking God to help him work things out.

He found a sergeant. "Sergeant, I am a Seventh-day Adventist, and I want to see about getting my Sabbaths free. Where do I go and who do I see?" Desmond asked.

"Sounds like you need to see the regimental chaplain. His name is Stanley, and you can find him at the chapel near the regimental aid station," answered the sergeant, not unkindly.

After receiving directions, Desmond found the aid station. "Is Chaplain Stanley here somewhere?" he asked.

"You will find him in the chapel right over there, soldier."

Desmond went to the chapel and saw a man sitting at a desk right inside the door. "Are you Chaplain Stanley, Sir?" On receiving an affirmative answer he continued, "I think you are the one I need to talk to."

"What is your name, and what do you want to talk to me about?" asked Chaplain Stanley.

"My name is Desmond T. Doss. I've just arrived in camp. Sir, I am a Seventh-day Adventist Christian, and I want to see if it will be possible for me to have Sabbaths free from duty. And I would like very much to have a pass so I can go to church in Columbia," Desmond answered politely.

"Glad to meet you, Doss. I have a good friend who is a Seventh-day Adventist. He is one of your ministers, I believe. Now as to your problem, I'm not sure what I can do for you because of the quarantine, but I can try," said the chaplain.

"You see, Sir, I have always gone to church, and I don't like to even think about staying away," remarked Desmond.

"OK. Thanks for coming. See me a little later in the week, and I'll see if I can work something out for you," the chaplain said as he dismissed Desmond.

Desmond could tell that Chaplain Stanley was a friendly and an understanding man, and he believed that he would help if he could. He was to have this opinion verified a number of times as the chaplain helped him with problems arising from his Seventh-day Adventist faith.

Desmond returned to Company M and soon settled into the routine of camp life. As near as he could tell, Company M seemed to be a company where at least some of the new soldiers were placed until the officers could tell where they would best fit in.

On Friday Desmond went to talk to Chaplain Stanley again. "Chaplain Stanley, what have you found out about my request for going to church tomorrow?" he asked.

"I'm glad you came, Doss. Our committee for such requests met, and we have decided to let you go to church tomorrow. The only problem is, you need to have someone to go with you."

Desmond was wondering who on earth he could get to go to church with him on Saturday, when he realized the chaplain was still talking. "But we have decided to just let you go by yourself," he finished.

Desmond picked up his pass at the aid station, and he was very happy to be going to church on that first Sabbath in camp. He enjoyed the services at the church. These people, who were so used to seeing soldiers come and go, greeted him warmly. He was even invited to stay for the potluck dinner for the soldiers who were there from other companies at Fort Jackson. At the end of that Sabbath, he had a very warm feeling and thanked God for the beautiful day.

Desmond was learning how an army is put together, with divisions, regiments, battalions, and companies. The medical department is a separate unit, not responsible to the company commanders, but responsible to the medical department. But the medics are divided up to be attached to each company. During the following week Desmond was transferred to the medical department as a medic, attached to B Company, of the 307th Regiment of the 77th Division.

The next Friday afternoon he found his way to the regimental aid station to see about getting a pass to go to church the next day. After the arrangements of the past week, he anticipated no trouble.

"Could I have a pass for tomorrow so that I can attend church?" Desmond asked the sergeant at the aid station.

"I guess you will have to get that from Captain Wendell (not his real name) if you want one. You know you new fellows are quarantined for two weeks, and I can't give you one," answered the sergeant.

"Where is he?" asked Desmond.

"He's gone right now, but he should be back in about fifteen minutes if you want to wait."

"I'll wait." Desmond knew it was important for him to see the captain.

Captain Wendell returned ten minutes later and saw Desmond seated in a chair. Desmond got up and saluted.

"What can I do for you, soldier?" the captain asked.

"Sir, my name is Desmond Doss, and I am a Seventh-day Adventist. Last week Chaplain Stanley was nice enough to make arrangements for me to go to church and also that I wouldn't have any work duties on Sabbath. It's my habit to go to church every week, and I would surely appreciate getting another pass."

"Wait a minute, Doss. I'm a Jew, and it is my habit to go to church each Sabbath, too—when I'm home. But we're in the army now. I have to work on Saturday, and you will have to do the same," remarked Captain Wendell.

"I'm sorry, Captain, but I can't look at it that way. My Bible says we are not to do any work on God's Sabbath, and I have to obey God. Chaplain Stanley said some sort of a committee met about me and decided I could go to church even though we're under quarantine. So could I have a pass for tomorrow?" asked Desmond.

"Guess I'll have to give you one if Stanley says so. Have the sergeant make it out, and I'll sign it," said Captain Wendell.

Desmond went happily on his way with his pass, knowing he would get to attend church the next day. He also remembered to thank God.

Each Friday afternoon Desmond faithfully went to the regimental aid station for his pass. Captain Wendell always fussed at him about his not working on Sabbath and about his wanting a pass for church, but he would finally give him the pass. Until one day . . .

"Doss, I'm tired of giving you a pass to go to church every week. I've already told you that you need to forget this Sabbath business while you are in the army and go to work like the rest of us. After all, you can have Sunday off. That should be enough," said the captain that Friday.

"Captain, Sir, I can't do that. I work on Sundays when I take Sabbaths off. But I just can't work on my Sabbath."

"Well, Doss, I'll give you a pass today, but don't come back again. I won't sign another pass for you, and I won't let anyone else sign a pass. Is that clear?" And Desmond knew he meant it.

"Doss, what time is your church out?" the captain continued.

"It gets out around noon, but there is usually a potluck dinner at the church for the soldiers," replied Desmond.

"Well, you be back here at camp by four. And report here to the aid station."

"Yes, Sir," agreed Desmond.

He went to church in a somewhat disturbed frame of mind the next day. When the time came for the morning prayer, Desmond explained the problem he was having to the people there and asked that they pray for him that he might be able to attend church regularly. They prayed for him at church and promised to pray for him during the week.

When Desmond returned to camp and reported to the aid station that afternoon, Captain Wendell was not there. "OK, Doss. You got back on time," said the sergeant. "Why don't you go over to the chapel for a while? We can call you if we need you."

Desmond wasn't sure what would happen if they needed him, but he would cross that bridge when the time came.

But at the chapel he found Chaplain Stanley, and it was a joy to talk to this friendly man of God.

"Hello, Doss. Good to see you. How are things going since you got in the medics?" questioned the chaplain.

"Not too bad, Chaplain Stanley. I'm really learning a lot, and I enjoy the work. But I did run into a problem today." And Desmond proceeded to tell the chaplain of his problems with the captain over the Sabbath and the pass.

"Desmond, I really want to help you out," offered Chaplain Stanley. "The only thing I know to do is take it to the division. Captain Wendell won't like it a bit, and he won't like me for doing it, but I don't see anything else to do. I'll do it and let you know how I come out."

Chaplain Stanley and Desmond visited for some time. Then at sunset and the close of his Sabbath, Desmond left after telling the chaplain how much he appreciated the help he had been giving him.

Friday Desmond again saw Chaplain Stanley. "Good news, Doss," said the chaplain. "The division has OK'd your Sabbath pass. Here is the paper on it. It says that Desmond Doss is to receive a pass to go to church on Saturday whenever it is at all possible. That should take care of things for you." Chaplain Stanley handed the paper to Desmond.

"You don't know how much I appreciate this, Chaplain," said Desmond. "God bless you, Sir."

That afternoon Desmond again made his way to the regimental aid station, bringing the division paper that Chaplain Stanley had given him. The sergeant saw him coming.

"I can't give you a pass, Doss," he said, "and the captain isn't here."

"It's a division order, Sergeant," said Desmond. "Where is Captain Wendell?"

"He is out in the field giving calisthenics to the men," answered the sergeant. This was something Desmond had never known the captain to do before.

"Well, you make out the pass, and I'll take it to him to sign," Desmond told the sergeant.

Desmond took the pass and went out to where the captain was. He saluted and then handed him the paper from the division and the pass.

"At ease," Captain Wendell told the men, as he took the paper and read it over. His face got red, but he did sign the pass that he had declared he would never sign—in front of all the men. From that time on, Desmond felt that the captain didn't like him, and Captain Wendell gave him reason to feel that way.

But again Desmond Doss went to church on Sabbath.

CHAPTER TEN

WEDDING BELLS

During the various problems he was having, particularly over the Sabbath, Desmond could always count on one person to stand by him and encourage him. That person was Dorothy. They were separated by many miles, but the postal service was available, and they made good use of it.

One Sabbath at church, Desmond was talking to Mrs. Thomas, one of the friendly church members. "How is everything going, Desmond?" she asked. "Is the army treating you right?"

"Well, yes, Mrs. Thomas," he answered. "Actually, I'm learning a lot of things in the army. Aside from having some trouble getting my pass to come to church, I haven't had too many problems. The only thing is, I get lonesome for my family, especially for Dorothy. You know she is my fiancée. We haven't seen each other since I was drafted."

"Desmond," Mrs. Thomas said, "is there any way Dorothy could come down here to see you? If so, she's welcome to stay at our house anytime she wants to."

Desmond's face lit up. "That would be wonderful, Mrs. Thomas. I'm not sure what we can work out, but we'll surely try."

Due to that invitation, Dorothy arrived in Columbia a few weeks later. The quarantine was over by this time, of course, so Desmond spent all the time he could with Dorothy during the weekend that she was there. The Thomases were very hospitable people and seemed to enjoy having the young people in their house.

Saturday night, Desmond and Dorothy were visiting in the living room. (The Thomases had discreetly moved to the dining room for the evening.) The young couple always enjoyed praying together, so they both prayed. Then Dorothy asked, "Desmond, how are things really going for you? Are you having any other problems besides the ones you've told me about in your letters?"

"Sweetheart, as far as the army goes, it isn't too bad. I'm making it. But I miss you so much, and I wish there were some way we could get married. I know you want to go to nursing school in September, and I don't want to keep you from that. But it would be so nice if we could get married and be together part of the time at least."

Dorothy sighed. "Honey, I've been thinking about this problem for a long time. I still would like to get my nurse's training, but I'm beginning to feel that you need me more than I need to be a nurse. Why don't we get married, but be very careful not to have any children until you get back from the war. What do you think?"

"Sweetheart! Do you really mean that? That would be so wonderful. You could come to wherever I might be stationed if we were married. And I could get as much time off as possible to be with you." The possibility brought a sparkle to Desmond's eyes. After a few hugs and kisses to seal this wonderful new idea, Desmond and Dorothy decided that perhaps they should make some definite plans.

"Let's get married in the Richmond church, honey," Dorothy suggested enthusiastically. "When can you get a furlough?"

"I'm in basic training, and I can't get a furlough before that is done. That will be in August, I think. I'll have to check on that and see if I can get a definite date for a furlough."

They looked at the calendar on the wall. It looked like they could have the ceremony about August 15 if all went well. Dorothy had to go back to Richmond on Sunday, but it was with comparatively light hearts that the couple said Goodbye as they parted.

Desmond went to Captain Wendell and asked about a furlough, but he couldn't get a definite date. "Officers and noncoms come first. You'll just have to wait your turn." Desmond wished he could tell Dorothy something specific, but they would just have to be patient, he decided. August was two months away still, anyway.

In 1942, July 4 came on Friday, and everyone at Fort Jackson was on vacation for that day. Desmond was lonesome to see his beloved Dorothy again; he had to find some way to see her! If he left for Richmond on the bus on Thursday night, he decided, and came back on Sunday in time for reveille on Monday morning, no one would know. He didn't tell anyone at the camp of his intentions. Fortunately, he did tell Mrs. Thomas that he planned to go see Dorothy for the weekend.

His plans were working very well. He arrived in Richmond and found his way to the Schutte home, anticipating a joyful surprise reunion with Dorothy. He knew she would be happy to see him. He knocked, hoping Dorothy would be the one to come to the door so he could see the happy, surprised look on her face. Instead, Mother Schutte answered the door. "Desmond! What are you doing here?" She was the one who looked surprised instead of Dorothy.

"Why, I came to see that sweet daughter of yours, Mother Schutte," Desmond replied.

"But . . . but, Desmond. Dorothy went to see you! She wanted to surprise you." Desmond could hardly believe his ears.

Now what do I do? he thought. Dorothy's mother was thinking the same thing. "Let's see," she said. "What is the name of the people where Dorothy stays when she goes down there? Isn't it Thomas? Why don't we call and ask Dorothy to come back here?" It was still early Friday morning, so what she was suggesting was possible.

In the meantime, Dorothy had arrived in Columbia, looking forward to the wonderful surprise Desmond would have when she saw her. She found her way to the Thomas home and knocked on the door. She wondered for a moment why Mrs. Thomas had such a surprised look on her face as she opened the door.

"Dorothy! What are you doing here?" Mrs. Thomas asked.

"I came to see Desmond. I wanted to surprise him," Dorothy answered.

"You'll surprise him, all right—if you can find him. He went to Richmond to surprise you, Dorothy!"

The truth of the situation dawned on Dorothy. "Oh, Mrs. Thomas, what shall I do?"

"Let's call and see if a train might be going back to Richmond soon," suggested Mrs. Thomas. A call to the train station told them that a train was leaving for Richmond in about twenty minutes. Dorothy practically ran to the station, arriving just in time to get on the train before it pulled out.

When Mother Schutte and Desmond called Mrs. Thomas, she could report that Dorothy was on her way back to Richmond. Desmond met her at the station, and they were able to spend a wonderful Sabbath together. But they decided they would never, never try to surprise each other that way again!

On Sunday, Desmond decided to take the train, rather than the bus, back to Fort Jackson because it would get him there at the right time. He would arrive in Columbia at 4:00 A.M. Monday, leaving enough time to get to Fort Jackson for reveille. The only problem was—the train broke down! Whatever was wrong was finally fixed, but as a result the train arrived in Columbia at noon, and Desmond didn't arrive at Fort Jackson until 1:00 P.M.—seven hours after reveille!

"Doss, where on earth were you at reveille this morning?" asked the sergeant when Desmond finally walked into his camp area. He didn't try to hide anything; he told the sergeant the whole story. His punishment was to spend the next ten evenings in the company aid station scrubbing the floor and straightening the shelves. And he couldn't go to the PX during this time.

It wasn't a particularly difficult punishment. He scrubbed the floor that had probably already been scrubbed during that day and did some straightening up. Then he had time to write to Dorothy and to his parents. Since he couldn't go to the PX himself, he asked a friend to take his uniform there to send it to the cleaners. *The best punishment I've ever had,* he decided. *Catch up on my letter writing and get my uniform cleaned for the wedding.*

The time when Desmond and Dorothy wanted to have their wedding was fast approaching. They needed to set a definite date, but Desmond hadn't been able to get a date for his furlough. Sergeant Ricky was on duty at the aid station when Desmond went once more to see about his furlough.

"Sergeant, what can I do about my furlough? You know that I told you I plan to get married, and I need to know when my furlough will come so Dorothy can set a definite date for the wedding," urged Desmond.

"Congratulations, Doss. I have one suggestion. Why don't you go to regimental headquarters and see the adjutant? He is the one who handles such things. Maybe he can give you a date," Sergeant Ricky suggested.

So Desmond went to regimental headquarters, but the adjutant wasn't in. As he stood momentarily, trying to decide his next move, the regimental commander came into the room. "What can I do for you, soldier?" he asked.

Saluting smartly, Desmond replied, "I needed to see the adjutant, Sir, but he isn't in. And I don't have permission to speak to you."

"Tell you what. I'll give you permission," the commander said kindly. "Now, what is it you need?"

"Sir, I want to get married when my basic training is finished. I have the girl and the church, but I haven't been able to get a furlough date so we can plan the wedding. I was wondering if somehow I could get a definite date for my furlough," Desmond answered.

"I don't think that is possible, Doss, because of OCS," the commander told him. When he saw the blank look on Desmond's face, he asked, "Aren't you lined up for officer candidate school?"

"No, Sir."

"Oh, that's different. Then I don't see why we can't set you a date. I'll call Captain Wendell." So saying, he picked up the phone and dialed the captain. "Wendell, I have Desmond Doss here in my office. He tells me he wants to get married. When a soldier wants to get married, you'd better let him go ahead and do it. Can you set up a definite date for his furlough so that he can make plans?"

Desmond was listening to the phone conversation, but he couldn't hear what Captain Wendell was saying, of course. When the commander hung up the phone, he turned to Desmond and said, "OK, Doss. Captain Wendell will fix you up. And, by the way, congratulations!"

"Thank you, Sir! And thank you for your help." Desmond smiled as he saluted once again.

When he arrived at the aid station, he started to go in to see Captain Wendell, but Sergeant Ricky stopped him. "Doss, don't you dare go in there! He'll take your head off. He's fuming mad! Why did you talk to the commander without permission?"

Desmond explained that the adjutant had not been in and that he hadn't talked to the commander—the commander had talked to him.

WEDDING BELLS

"Well, go on back to your barracks. I'll try to straighten the whole thing out with Captain Wendell. You can get your furlough date later when he's calmed down."

Desmond finally found that his furlough would start on Thursday, August 13. That would make it possible for he and Dorothy to get married on Saturday night, August 15, as they had hoped.

He arrived in Richmond on Thursday night. Friday, he and Dorothy went to the courthouse to get the marriage license. But there were complications. They learned that they both must have a blood test. They could have the test done that day, but the results wouldn't come back until Monday morning. No blood test, no marriage license until Monday! So no marriage until Monday, either.

On Monday morning they picked up their marriage license at the courthouse. The wedding would take place at 4:00 P.M. The church members were all interested in helping the young couple have a nice wedding; many were giving flowers to decorate the church. Desmond used Mother Schutte's car to go to the various homes to pick up the flowers. He took the flowers to the church and decided that he simply must have a haircut in order to look neat for the wedding. When he arrived at the barbershop, there was a line ahead of him. He decided he had time to wait. As he was waiting in line, a man came through the door wanting to know whose Ford was out in front of the barbershop.

"That's mine," Desmond volunteered. "Why?"

"It has a flat tire. I thought you might like to know," the man answered.

The barber had already learned that Desmond wanted a haircut because he was getting married later that afternoon. "Go ahead and fix the tire, soldier," he said. "I'll hold your place in line."

So Desmond fixed the tire and got his haircut and still managed to get back to the church in time to get ready for the wedding!

The wedding went off nicely. The groom was happy, and the bride was glowing. The ceremony was a little different from most. Instead of asking the bride and groom to say, "I do," the minister asked them to clasp hands if they wanted to be married for better, for worse, for richer, for poorer, etc.

In his prayer, the minister asked that the Lord would bless the young couple in a special way and that He would keep them both safe, even in war time.

At last they were Mr. and Mrs. Desmond T. Doss!

Desmond decided that the phrase, "for poorer," in their wedding ceremony was very appropriate. Twenty-one dollars a month didn't go very far, and Dorothy had no great amount of money either. They spent their wedding night at Desmond's parents' home in Lynchburg—as well as the few additional days and nights they had before Desmond had to go back to Fort Jackson.

Desmond did find that when he was married, his army pay increased a whole dollar a month—to twenty-two dollars—and that Dorothy would receive another fifty dollars a month. She worked whenever and wherever she could as she followed Desmond and lived near the camps where he was stationed—as did so many other wives during World War II. Dorothy tried to save all of the fifty dollars she received each month so that they would have a little nest egg when the war was over.

When Desmond's furlough was over and he returned to Fort Jackson, he hated to leave his new wife. But he was happy they were married. It gave him a feeling of stability as well as responsibility. He thanked the Lord that he had a wonderful wife to encourage him and to be with him—part of the time, at least.

CHAPTER ELEVEN

FORT JACKSON AND POINTS WEST

When Desmond returned to Fort Jackson after his furlough, he began to hear rumors that his unit would be shipping out soon. Where? Perhaps some knew, but most of the soldiers had no idea.

On September 10, 1942, the 77th Division left on a troop train for Fort Sill, Oklahoma. The camp was located near the small town of Lawton. Desmond soon found the Seventh-day Adventist church in town, and along with several other soldiers, he got passes to go to church on Sabbath mornings. Every Sabbath, the church ladies put on a fellowship dinner—sometimes called a potluck dinner. The soldiers always liked the good food they ate there.

But one lady in the church went the second—or maybe even the third and fourth—mile. Her name was Lovey Hutchinson, a very appropriate name. Desmond and the other soldiers never forgot her kindness. She would tell the soldier boys, "I work every day, but I never lock the door to my house. You boys are welcome to come in anytime you're in town. And I try to have food in the refrigerator all the time—if too many of you don't raid my refrigerator at the same time! You're welcome to help yourselves."

This did wonders for the soldiers' morale, and they took advantage of her kindness. Her home became a sort of private USO. Many times Lovey and the soldiers would pitch in together to cook a meal. They loved it!

After a couple of months at Fort Sill, the 77th Division reversed direction and spent a couple of days on a troop train going back to Fort Jackson. The troops spent the next two and a half months there mostly on maneuvers, usually involving hikes of twenty-five miles!

Desmond, of course, went along with the other men. One of the bad things to happen to the hikers was blisters.

"Doss, I need some help. My feet are killing me. Have you got anything for a blister?" Various soldiers would approach Desmond for help. He would prick the blister with a needle disinfected in alcohol, squeeze out the liquid, put a doughnut of gauze around the blister, and bandage it. That would take off the pressure and make it possible for the man to walk without hurting so much.

Desmond was kind of proud of his work in fixing up blisters. None of them ever got infected. As he worked on them, he wondered at times if what his teacher had said about doing things right the first time might apply even to fixing blisters.

When the soldiers were out on maneuvers, it would sometimes cause problems for Desmond and his Sabbath observance. "Could I have a pass so I can go to church tomorrow?" he asked the captain.

"Doss, we have no idea where we will be tomorrow night. How would you get back to us?" the captain replied.

"I don't know for sure, Captain. But if you will tell me approximately where you will be, I can probably find you. I believe God will help me."

"The trouble is, I don't know even approximately where we will be." But the captain did finally give Desmond a pass.

After spending a wonderful day with his church family, Desmond went back to camp to see if he could find a ride out to where the soldiers were on maneuvers. He finally found an MP who told him to go to a certain building where he would find army vehicles going out to the troops in the field. But when he arrived at the building and asked the MP in charge if anyone was going out to the troops that night, he received a negative answer. He started to walk away.

The MP stopped him. "You're not going anywhere, Private. You're under arrest. You can go out tomorrow with the rest of the prisoners."

What else could Desmond do? The next day when he arrived, along with the other prisoners, at the location where his company was posted, there was the inevitable teasing. "What kind of mischief have you been up to, Doss?" a number of soldiers wanted to know. "Did you get drunk?"

"No, all I did was go to church," Desmond answered innocently.

FORT JACKSON AND POINTS WEST

Time passed quickly, and once again Desmond's unit was on a troop train, this time heading for Louisiana and more maneuvers. This camp was different from anything they had experienced so far. For one thing, the camp was new; it was located in an area where no camp had ever been before. And it was wild country, including wild pigs, which were plentiful. They ran around the camp, even crawling into the tents with the soldiers at times. They managed to get into the food tent and helped themselves. Another new annoyance to the men were ticks and chiggers—plentiful in the south. A lot of scratching went on during those days!

While Desmond was in Louisiana, he was very happy to have Dorothy join him for a while. She found a room in a farmhouse just across the road from the camp. She and Desmond thanked the Lord that they could be together once more.

One Friday afternoon, Desmond asked Major Wendell (Captain Wendell had been promoted) for a pass to go to church the next day. The Major flatly refused. Desmond and Dorothy were disappointed, but they decided they would keep the Sabbath together anyway. Desmond went to the farmhouse the next morning to pick up Dorothy, and they spent the day out in the cow pasture, reading their Bibles, singing, and visiting. When he arrived back at camp that evening, he was told the Major wanted to see him—pronto!

"Private Doss reporting, Sir," Desmond said.

"What's the idea, Doss?" growled the Major. "I didn't give you a pass, but you went off to town anyway."

"I haven't been to town at all, Sir," replied Desmond. "My wife is living across the road, and we spent the day in the cow pasture there. Sir, may I remind you that it was a division order that I'm to have my Sabbaths off whenever that is at all possible?"

That took the wind out of the Major's sails, but he had to have a parting shot. "If I ever get half a chance, Doss, I'm going to court-martial you."

"Sir, I will try never to give you that half a chance," said Desmond.

★ ★ ★ ★ ★

The next place the 77th Division found itself was in the desert of Arizona. The division arrived there in April 1943 and spent a very hot summer, leaving in September. Again, they were in a place that had not been

73

a camp before. There were no air-cooled barracks. In fact, there were no barracks at all. Tents were set up on the hot sand. It was 110 to 120 degrees in the shade—except there was no shade!

Everything was hot, even the drinking water. It came from deep wells, but it was hot by the time it got to the men. To make it even more insipid, someone decided that the water should have salt in it because so many men were passing out with heat exhaustion. They also issued salt tablets to the men. The men needed the water, and they drank it—but not because they liked the hot, salty water. In fact, it often made them sick at their stomachs.

Once in a while, a load of beer was brought into the camp. The beer was surrounded with ice to keep it cool. How much the men would have enjoyed having some of the ice to put in the hot water to cool it down! The ice had pretty well melted by the time it reached camp, but the men were not allowed to have any that remained. After all, it was to keep the beer cold!

Sad to say, many soldiers who had never taken a drink of beer before started drinking it because it was the only cool beverage on the desert. They formed a habit they never stopped.

One day the soldiers were called together. "We're going on maneuvers today to Montezuma's Head. Get your gear together. You can take a canteen of water; that should last you until we get to the end of our twelve-mile hike. You'll be given lunch there and water to put in your canteens for the return hike."

There was quite a bit a grumbling. Twelve miles in cool weather with a breeze blowing would have been hard enough, but in this scorching weather, it was murder! If fact, for some, it almost was.

Desmond went with everyone else, of course. But when he got to the end of the twelve-mile hike, there was no water for him to fill his empty canteen. The water had been brought out in barrels, but much of it was used to make coffee and tea, which he didn't drink. There wasn't enough plain water to go around, so he and a few others didn't receive their water allotment.

Desmond and another soldier started back with no water. Before long, his companion slumped forward on the ground. Desmond recognized the signs of heat exhaustion, but he hardly knew how to treat him. What the soldier needed was water—and neither of them had any.

FORT JACKSON AND POINTS WEST

About that time, the regimental commander came along and so did a jeep. They loaded the unconscious soldier into the jeep.

"Sir, can we have some water? We didn't get any before we started back, and that's the reason this soldier passed out," Desmond asked.

"You're lying, soldier, and you know it. You just drank it all up, and now you want more," was the commander's cruel reply.

"No, Sir. We didn't get any," Desmond insisted.

At that, the commander dumped some of the water from his canteen onto the unconscious solder, not even trying to get it into his mouth where it was needed.

"Sir, may I have some water?" Desmond pleaded.

"Here, you can have a swig," the commander answered.

Desmond put the canteen to his lips and took a drink—a big one—until the commander grabbed the canteen from him. "That's enough. Now your friend will have to go back on the jeep, but you'll walk. You hear me?" ordered the commander.

The commander left, and against orders, Desmond jumped on the jeep and tried to shade the unconscious soldier. He realized that he, too, could easily pass out without water if he tried to walk back—and he didn't want to become a casualty out there in the desert. The jeep came to an aid station where there was some water. Desmond had a good drink and then filled his canteen. After that, he walked the rest of the way with no trouble. He never learned what happened to the unconscious soldier.

★ ★ ★ ★ ★

The desert camp was set up some miles west of Phoenix, Arizona. Between Phoenix and the camp was a small town—Buckeye. Desmond soon found a Seventh-day Adventist church in Buckeye. He also found it was not easy to get to the little town.

One Sabbath, he learned of a convoy of army trucks going through Buckeye. He asked one of the drivers if it would be possible for him to ride to the town. "Tell you what, Doss. I'm not supposed to take anyone to Buckeye, but get in the back of my truck. When you get to where you want off, rap on the roof of the truck. I'll develop engine trouble for a minute while you jump off. But remember, if you get caught, I don't know anything about it."

Desmond rapped on the truck roof. The driver pulled over and jumped out to raise the hood for a minute. Then he jumped back in the truck. Meantime, Desmond was over the side and behind a building. He made it to church that time easily, but he knew it wouldn't happen like that often.

There was a small flag-stop train station near the camp. A soldier could get on that train, and it stopped in Buckeye. But some of the soldiers—probably after imbibing some of that free beer—had caused a lot of trouble on the train, so no soldiers, not even generals, were allowed to board the train at the camp.

So there was only one sure way Desmond could get to church. That was to go to Phoenix in an army vehicle and catch the train back to Buckeye. But by the time he could accomplish all that and arrive in Buckeye, church would be over.

So Desmond went to see the stationmaster at the flag-stop station. "Sir," he said. "I am a Seventh-day Adventist, and I want to go to church in Buckeye on Saturday morning. I know we are not supposed to board the train here, but do you think I could possibly board your train and go to Buckeye—just so I can go to church and nowhere else?"

"Soldier, my superiors don't forbid me to let a soldier on the train, and if you are going to church, I think we can depend on you not to make a ruckus. Yes, you can get on the train," said the stationmaster.

"Every Saturday morning?" asked Desmond.

"Yes, every Saturday morning," he answered.

"Thank you, Sir," said Desmond. So each Sabbath morning, Desmond boarded the train for Buckeye and church. This didn't go over so well with his superiors at camp. One of them remarked, "Doss gets more passes than the general."

Another reason Desmond was so anxious to go to church was that Dorothy was in Arizona, too. She was working for a doctor in Buckeye, so he not only got to go to church—he got to go to church with Dorothy! Sabbaths became special days for them.

★ ★ ★ ★ ★

One Friday afternoon when Desmond went to the hot headquarters tent of the medical battalion to pick up his usual Sabbath pass, he sensed that something was going on that he did not quite understand. The top sergeant, who reflected the commanding officer's disapproval of Doss, handed over the pass with an unpleasant grin.

"I won't be doing this much longer, Doss," he said. "Arrangements are being made so you can have all your Saturdays off from now on."

Desmond decided he would find out what this was all about so he found an officer of his battalion and asked him what was going on.

"I've got good news for you, Doss," he said. "You're getting out of the army. We've discussed your case at length and have come to the conclusion that you are eligible for a Section Eight discharge. Go to your tent until the discharge committee is ready to see you. It won't be long."

Desmond was human. He had had enough of the hot desert. His nose was swollen and inflamed from the constant dust; his eyes were watering. The officers were down on him, and he could never relax. He had had enough. He was ready to get out of the army and go home.

But he knew that Section Eight referred to mental instability. And Desmond Doss did not believe that he was a "nut" just because he wanted to go to church on Saturday.

The discharge committee soon called him to appear before it. The committee consisted of five medical officers and the battalion commander; they were sitting around a table out in the open in the heat of the desert. The chairman of the committee told Desmond he was up for a discharge, based on Section Eight—a fact he already knew.

"Why Section Eight? Isn't my work satisfactory?" asked Desmond. He was facing five medical officers who thought he was crazy. What could he say?

"Well, yes it is," admitted the officer. "We have no problem with your work. It is just that you are too strict in your religion. Being off on Saturday could mean that you might miss something important you should know."

"Sir," said Desmond, "if I serve God on His Sabbath as He commands in the fourth commandment, I feel He will give me wisdom when I need it. If it is an emergency, I'm always ready to take care of sick or hurt soldiers on the Sabbath. Another medic and I have worked it out so that he takes care of my duties on Sabbath, and I take care of his duties on Sunday. May I remind you, Sir, that Company B has the lowest number of men on sick call in the whole regiment?"

/

Desmond might as well have saved his breath. All the committee was interested in was for Desmond to accept the discharge without protest. This he could not do.

"You say my work is satisfactory," he reminded the committee, "so the only ground you have for my discharge is my keeping the seventh-day Sabbath. I'd be a very poor Christian if I accepted a discharge implying that I was mentally unbalanced because of my religion. I'm sorry, gentlemen, but I can't accept that kind of discharge."

That answer stopped the Section Eight discharge. It was obvious that Washington would never approve a discharge given purely on religious grounds. So Desmond remained in the army on the hot desert. It was a strange victory, and one that did not increase his popularity with the brass.

It began to be hinted that the division was going to move out of the desert—a welcome hint. No more hot desert sand, no more warm water to drink, no more desert maneuvers. The division was ready to move on.

A couple of days after the Section Eight committee meeting, Desmond was told to report to the regimental aid station headquarters. He wondered why, but soon found out. "Doss, you are being transferred to the infantry," the sergeant told him. His enemies in the medical battalion had found another way to get rid of him. He was to turn in his medical equipment and report to the First Battalion Headquarters Company.

As he was collecting his medical equipment, he realized his troubles were beginning. He bowed his head for a moment and prayed, "Dear Jesus, please be with me and help me to know what to do." The thought came to him to go see Chaplain Stanley, who was now the division chaplain. The chaplain listened to his story and was sympathetic, but there was little he could do at that point.

Desmond turned in his medical gear. As he was leaving his tent, a friend, T/4 March Howell, told him goodbye. "By the way, Doss," he said, "I just made a ten-dollar bet with your new company commander. He said he'd have you carrying a gun in thirty days. I bet him he wouldn't."

"Howell, you know I don't believe in gambling. I don't know how to make both of you win, but you know I won't carry a gun," said Desmond.

Desmond reported in to his new commander, Captain Cosner (not his real name). Cosner had been warned about this troublemaker who was being transferred to his company, and he was ready for Doss. He had assigned Desmond to the pioneer ammunition section; the carbine he was to carry was ready for him.

"Here, Doss," he ordered. "Take this carbine."

Desmond realized what the lieutenant was trying to do. As a conscientious objector, he was officially exempt from bearing arms, but he was not exempt from obeying the direct order of a commissioned officer.

So Desmond did not take the carbine, but replied, "I'm sorry, Sir, but according to my religious convictions, I cannot bear arms."

The captain tried again with the carbine and then tried the same game with a .45 automatic pistol. "Here, Doss, you can take this. It isn't really a weapon."

"Then what is it, Sir?" asked Desmond. The captain tried with a trench knife and an ammunition kit. Desmond declined to take these as well, but without making a direct refusal.

"Look, Doss," said the captain. "I don't want you to kill anyone. I just want you to train like the rest of the soldiers."

"I would rather put my trust in the Lord than in a carbine," said Desmond.

The captain tried something else. "Doss, you're married. Suppose someone was raping your wife. Wouldn't you use a gun?"

"I wouldn't have one," replied Desmond.

"What would you do, then?"

"I wouldn't just stand there," said Desmond, sharply. "I wouldn't kill, and I wouldn't use a gun, but he'd sure wish he were dead by the time I got through with him!"

That ended the conflict for that day. By the way, at the end of thirty days, it is presumed T/4 Howell collected the ten dollars.

CHAPTER TWELVE

POINTS EAST AGAIN AND ON TO COMBAT

The time had come for the soldiers to board the troop train for the trip to Indiantown Gap Military Reservation in Pennsylvania. It is doubtful if even one soldier would have wanted to stay out in the desert—they were all ready to find a cool spot. They had almost forgotten what cool air felt like. They didn't know it then, but the time would come later when just a little of that hot desert air would have felt good.

The troop train wound its way across the United States and arrived in Indiantown Gap. Here Captain Cosner had the last word in the conflict with Desmond over the bearing of arms. He put Desmond on permanent KP, and he was given the job of scrubbing the pots and pans and washing the tables. Lye was put in the water for these jobs, and Desmond's hands became sore and raw and bleeding. He couldn't touch anything without his hands hurting.

When Desmond left the Arizona desert, Dorothy also came back home to Richmond, Virginia. But since Desmond could not even get a pass to leave the camp area, there was no use for her to come up to Pennsylvania and live near the camp.

★ ★ ★ ★ ★

"Here's a letter for you, Doss." The sergeant tossed the letter to Desmond as he was returning to the barracks one evening.

Desmond was happy to receive a letter from his mother and dad. But the message of the letter was rather disconcerting. "Harold will be home on furlough from the navy starting on the twelfth. Is there any chance you could get a furlough, too, so that we could all be together before Harold goes overseas? He'll be here for a week."

Desmond looked at the calendar and found that he would have to leave in just three or four days if he were to see his brother. Desmond and several other soldiers were due to have a furlough, so he felt he could get one in time to see Harold. The next day Captain Cosner called these men together to give them their furlough papers. He was passing them out when he came to Desmond.

"Doss, you haven't qualified with a weapon yet," he said. "There's a regulation that you can't have a furlough unless you qualify with a weapon." So saying he grabbed the paper back from Desmond and tore it up.

What a disappointment! Desmond went to the chaplain and then to other officers and finally to the commander of the regiment.

"Sir," said Desmond. "I'm a CO, and I'm supposed to be exempt from bearing arms. But because I can't bear arms, my company captain won't give me a furlough so I can go home and see my brother before he goes overseas. Could you help me?"

"Doss, you come from Virginia, don't you? There are a lot of good army men who have come from Virginia. You should follow their example. Sounds to me like you are a goldbrick and a shirker," said the commander. "Why don't you forget all this CO business and take a gun like the rest of the infantry? Doss, this is just a friendly chat, trying to get you to see things differently."

"Sir, I haven't had a chance to say a word," said Desmond. If this was a friendly chat, he wondered what an unfriendly one would be.

"No, I will not give you a furlough. You don't deserve it. You're dismissed," said the commander.

So Desmond went sadly to the telephone in the post exchange to call home long distance. When his mother answered the phone, he said, "Mom, this is Desmond. I got your letter, but I can't come home." Then he choked up. At that moment he wondered if he would see Harold or even his folks again. The way things were going, he might wind up in prison. He stood there not able to speak, while the seconds he was paying for slipped by.

"Desmond, what's the matter?" asked his mother. "Where are you? Desmond!"

Desmond finally got control of his emotions enough to explain the situation to his mother. She was so sorry, but didn't know what to tell him to do. But it did help him to hear his mother's voice.

Next morning he was in the camp kitchen, with his hands and arms deep in the soap suds, when a fellow soldier came in.

"Doss, the sergeant told me to tell you to report to the medical battalion headquarters."

Now what? thought Desmond as he dried his hands on the rough towel.

When he arrived at the medical battalion headquarters, Major Wendell said, "Welcome back, Doss. You're in the medics again."

Desmond could hardly believe it, and he wondered why the sudden change, but he did have the presence of mind to ask the sergeant standing nearby, "Can I have my furlough?" He went on to explain about his brother being home for a few days before going overseas.

"No, you will have to wait your turn for a furlough," the sergeant said.

"Can I have a pass then?" he asked.

"If you have a pass, you can't have a furlough."

"I have no choice in the matter. Give me the pass, please," said Desmond.

He went on home that very day. Next morning he found out what had happened. When his parents received his phone call, they sent a night letter to Carlyle B. Haynes, chairman of the Seventh-day Adventist Church's War Service Commission in Washington, D.C., telling him about Desmond and his problems.

Next morning, Haynes called the regimental commander at Indiantown Gap. "I understand you are having some difficulty with a soldier named Desmond Doss. Is it necessary for me to come up there to investigate?"

"Oh, no, Mr. Haynes. It is just a little misunderstanding. We have it all straightened out," answered the commander. That was when Desmond was suddenly transferred back to the medical battalion.

Actually, the commander, and those under him who had caused Desmond trouble, realized they would be in trouble if Carlyle B. Haynes came to their camp to investigate. Desmond was a conscientious objector and was not to be forced to bear arms. Desmond had even seen on the commander's desk a letter that he knew was in his own files—a letter signed by President Roosevelt, commander in chief, and George C. Marshall, chief of staff, saying that conscientious objectors could not be forced to bear arms. So Desmond knew that the commander was aware of this regulation and that he also knew that he and others would be in trouble if Carlyle B. Haynes did any investigating.

As Desmond saw impossible situations being resolved in his favor, he realized that God was working things out for him. And he always remembered to thank God for the wonderful ways He took care of him.

★ ★ ★ ★ ★

The 77th Division trained in the whole area. They were at Indiantown Gap, but also at Camp Pickett in Virginia, and up in the mountains near Elkins, West Virginia. When they were taken up into the mountains, they were wearing khakis. By the time they reached their destination, there was seven inches of snow on the ground. That was when they wished they had just a little of that Arizona desert heat!

One thing happened in the mountains that was significant to Desmond's later military career, although he didn't realize it at the time. One important thing the soldiers worked on was tying knots. They had to evacuate each other over cliffs, across streams, and out of trees—and their lives could depend on knowing how to tie a good knot. Desmond had learned to tie knots in his Junior Missionary Volunteer program at church school, and he liked tying knots.

"Doss, you are pretty good at knot tying. Why don't you help some of the others learn to tie knots?" said his sergeant one day. Desmond was happy to do it.

One day he had men practicing on each end of a long rope. They were doing fine, and he wanted to practice tying the bowline knot himself. So he made an end by doubling the rope in the middle and tied a bowline knot. He found he had two loops instead of one, and they both held firmly. He had never seen this done before, and he decided to remember it in case he ever needed it.

★ ★ ★ ★ ★

The 77th Division, the Statue of Liberty Division, had been training together in the United States for a little over two years. Their training had been thorough, and they worked together as a good team. The time had come for them to put this training to use in World War II.

The troops were at Camp Pickett, Virginia. "Where do you suppose we will be sent?" the soldiers asked each other. No one knew. It could be the European theater of war or away off in the Pacific theater.

One day the whole outfit was called together. "Get your things together for travel," they were told. "We'll be pulling out day after tomorrow."

Wives were permitted to come to the camp area to see their husbands off, so Dorothy came from Richmond very early on the morning the division was to move out. It was good to be together, even if they could only hold hands and whisper "I love you" as they waited for the train.

"All aboard!" One last kiss, and Desmond boarded the train with the other soldiers. He sat at a window where he could wave goodbye to his Dorothy.

As the train started west, Desmond was told to report to the baggage car to help peel potatoes—a never-ending job in the army. He began to recognize landmarks that showed him the train would soon go through his home town of Lynchburg. He knew the train would pass very near his parents' home on Easley Avenue. He also knew his father liked to watch trains go by.

"Hey, guys, he told the soldiers working with him. "We are about to go past my home, and my dad always likes to watch the trains go by. Come help me wave to him." So the boys collected mops, brooms, and dust pans and stood at the open doorway of the train. As they came in sight of the man standing on his front porch, they started waving the various items at him. He probably wondered what it was all about, never dreaming that one of the soldiers was his own son.

Desmond did something else. He found a piece of paper and wrote on it, "We're shipping out. Pray for me. Love, Desmond." Then he tied the handkerchief he had used to wave goodbye to Dorothy around the rolled-up paper and tossed it off the train. His folks received the paper with the message—the next day.

Desmond was feeling pretty down at that moment. He felt he was leaving all that was near and dear to him. As the train crossed over the long trestle in the center of Lynchburg, the thought crossed his mind that he might as well jump off and end his troubles. But he realized that would be taking his own life and would be breaking the sixth commandment, so he said a short prayer to his God and went back to peeling spuds.

As the train rolled down the tracks, the soldiers began to realize that they were heading west—which would eventually mean the Pacific theater of war. Three days later they pulled into Oakland, California. From there they transferred to the troop ship that would take them under the Golden Gate Bridge and across the Pacific Ocean.

"Never thought I would see the Hawaiian Islands," remarked another soldier as he and Desmond were standing together on the deck of the troop ship after it landed in Honolulu.

"Neither did I," said Desmond. "I guess this is Pearl Harbor where the Japanese dropped their bombs."

The division was taken up into the hills at the opposite end of the island from Honolulu, where they set up camp. On the first Thursday night, Desmond was sitting on his bunk, writing a letter to Dorothy. All of a sudden he seemed to hear a voice saying, "Go to the air force base." He ignored it. Again the message came. He didn't understand what it was all about, but he put the letter away and went to the aid station.

"May I have a pass to go to the air force base?" he asked.

"Know somebody there?" asked the sergeant.

"No."

"Well, I sure don't know why you want to go, but go ahead. But be back by ten-thirty," the sergeant said as he handed him the pass.

Desmond didn't even know where the air force base was. He started down the dirt road to the highway, but didn't know which direction to go when he got there. He turned right, and soon an army jeep picked him up. "Where are you going?" the driver asked.

"To the air force base," answered Desmond.

"Soldier, you had better get out and go the other direction, then."

Desmond did get out and eventually found the air force base.

He decided he would go to the office and see if there were any Seventh-day Adventists on the base.

He asked, "Do you have any Seventh-day Adventists here?"

DESMOND DOSS

"Sure don't know of any. Tell you what, soldier. Why don't you go to the aid station over there? They might be able to help you."

Desmond found his way to the aid station, but asked his question a little differently this time. "Is there anyone here who leaves every Saturday morning to go to church?"

"I don't know of any," replied the attendant.

Right then an officer came in. He had heard the conversation. "Warm goes someplace every Saturday morning. Maybe he's the one you want to see. He works in the dental office right over there."

Desmond found Corporal Warm. Yes, he was a Seventh-day Adventist. Yes, he knew where the church was in Honolulu and went there every Sabbath. The two of them had a good visit and agreed that Desmond would come to meet Warm on Sabbath and go to church with him.

As Desmond left, he looked at his watch. Ten-fifteen! He'd never get back by ten thirty. It was after ten-forty-five when he arrived at the camp gate.

"Halt! Who goes there?" asked the guard.

"Private Doss, Sir," answered Desmond.

"Doss, what in the world are you doing here at this time of night?"

"I had a pass to go to the air force base, and it took longer than I thought it would. I'm sorry," apologized Desmond.

"Well, beat it back to your tent, and don't get caught or we'll both be in trouble."

When Desmond went to the aid station to pick up his Sabbath pass on Friday, the sergeant was on duty. Desmond politely asked for a pass so he could go to church.

"Doss, isn't there any place on earth where the Adventists don't have a church?" asked the sergeant humorously.

"Not very many places, Sergeant. We have them all over the world," answered Desmond.

Desmond and Corporal Warm had a very enjoyable day with the church members in Honolulu. Desmond got to meet other soldiers, navy men, and air force men there also. He met a civilian chaplain who took good care of "his boys." "Dad" Munson was well liked by the boys, too. They enjoyed the chalk talks he gave occasionally. One picture he drew was of a medical soldier taking care of a wounded soldier, with Christ looking down with approval. Desmond really liked that picture, and a few years later, "Dad" Munson painted a picture of that scene for him to use with the talks he gave.

★ ★ ★ ★ ★

Before long the 77th Division was getting ready to leave Hawaii with its wonderful weather, its friendly people, and its tasty pineapples. This time the troop ship they boarded was going farther west. Again the soldiers did not know their destination.

It was on this ship, as they sailed out of Hawaii, that Desmond spent several evenings on deck remembering what had happened to him as he grew up.

CHAPTER THIRTEEN

GUAM AND LEYTE

On July 9, 1944, the convoy of troop ships sailed out of Pearl Harbor, again heading in a westerly direction. The 77th Statue of Liberty Division was on board. Destroyers were accompanying the ships, and the whole convoy was zigzagging as it attempted to stop any kind of surprise attack from the Japanese at sea.

Several days later the convoy crossed the International Date Line, and in a few more days arrived at the Eniwetok Atoll in the Marshall Islands. There the group received official orders to proceed to Guam. For the first time the whole division would take part in actual combat.

"I don't know whether to be scared or excited," Desmond remarked to a fellow soldier one day.

"Both," he said.

The war that had started on December 7, 1941, with the bombing of Pearl Harbor in Hawaii, was now in its third year. It is no secret that America was not prepared for war on December 7, 1941. But right away the whole country was thrust into a hurry-up war machine. Ships, tanks, vehicles, and ammunition of all kinds had to be manufactured, and men had to be trained for army, navy, marine, and air force service. The draft system was initiated—"You go to war whether you want to or not." People lived with the rationing of sugar, shortening, gasoline, and other items.

The Japanese, besides bombing Pearl Harbor, quickly conquered Guam, the Philippines, Iwo Jima, and other Pacific islands. Two and a half years later, the Americans were beginning to free these islands one at a time. It wasn't easy! The Japanese were well dug in and intended to stay where they were. It took a lot of hard fighting to convince them otherwise. Many military men were killed, and many more were wounded. Desmond was one of the medics who cared for these men.

Much later Desmond heard an intriguing story. He never knew for sure that it was true. It could have been. A Seventh-day Adventist minister realized that he was being followed. One day his "shadow" approached him.

"Sir, do you know anything about Guam?" the stranger asked the minister.

"Well, yes, I do," he answered.

"General MacArthur would like to talk to you. Would you be so kind as to come with me to see him?" the man asked.

When they arrived at the general's headquarters, he asked, "What do you know about Guam? If you were to land on Guam to fight the Japanese, where would you do it?"

"There is only one place, Sir—Agat Bay. There are too many steep cliffs on the rest of the island. But I warn you, Agat Bay is heavily fortified. The Japanese are well dug in," the minister answered.

After looking over a map of Guam and discussing the whole situation, General MacArthur asked, "How do you know so much about Guam?"

"General, I was a Seventh-day Adventist missionary there for many years. I became well acquainted with the whole island while I was there. We Americans had to leave when Japan conquered Guam."

So the 77th Division was now at Agat Bay.

★ ★ ★ ★ ★

"Sorry we can't get in any closer, fellows," the sailors on the ships told the soldiers. "It's too shallow in the bay."

The soldiers were given plenty of ammunition, but they had to carry it above their heads as they slipped into water that came up to their arm pits. Desmond didn't have ammunition, of course, but he had plenty of first aid supplies and bandages to carry and keep from getting wet. The men finally got to shore, not knowing what to expect.

One thing they hadn't realized about Guam was its rain. Rain, rain, and RAIN! When they got to the shore, the rain had turned the dirt into soupy mud. As the soldiers made their way farther up into the hills, the soupy mud turned to sticky mud. Soldiers are supposed to be tall and look sharp in their uniforms, aren't they? That is the picture most people have. These soldiers looked anything but sharp in their wet, muddy uniforms. Their reaction was to use all the curse words they could bring to mind as they sloshed through the mud.

Desmond thought there was a better way. "Onward, Christian soldiers," he sang softly to himself as he also sloshed through the sometimes knee-deep mud.

"Here are your K rations, gang. Enough to last for three days—until we take Barrigada," said the lieutenant. "Do you know why that is an important objective?"

"No, Sir. Why?" asked several soldiers.

"There is a real good well there. You fellows have been drinking what water you could get. Even with the purification tablets, a lot of you have been sick at your stomachs and had diarrhea. Good water will help, I think."

The K rations were mostly beans and bacon, or bacon and cheese. Since Desmond was a vegetarian who especially did not eat pork products because of what he had read in Leviticus 11, he had little to eat except hard "dog biscuits" and an occasional coconut from a tree. Whether it was true or not, the soldiers believed the "dog biscuits" and C and K rations were leftovers from World War I.

The first night ashore, they dug muddy foxholes to spend the night. They appreciated the fact that a cannon was blasting away at the Japanese in the hills behind them, but the noise was terrific, and they felt they were being blasted out of their foxholes. None of the soldiers remembers getting any sleep that night.

The next day the soldiers were keeping a sharp eye out for their enemies. They saw some soldiers just a short distance away! They opened fire, and the enemy returned the fire—until they all suddenly realized both groups were Americans! That battle was stopped before it got started—or at least before anyone was hurt.

A little later as they were walking down a road, they saw a church in flames. They learned that the Japanese had been using the church as an ammunition dump and headquarters building. The Americans had bombed the building, and the ammunition inside was exploding as it burned. Fortunately it was far enough away that there was little chance of any of the men being wounded or killed by the exploding ammunition.

Next day they went on toward Barrigada, but with Japanese snipers—and occasionally a tank or a foxhole with machine guns—it took them longer to get to Barrigada than they expected.

The soldiers began to complain of hunger, including Desmond. They finally reached their objective and found themselves linked up with a marine unit. At this place the marines had good food; they weren't depending on C or K rations. So they had thrown their rations on the junk pile. The promised food that the marines were to fix for them wasn't ready, but the cast-off C and K rations were right there. Many of the soldiers picked up a can or two of the rations to eat while they waited. They were hungry! Desmond found something he could eat and did the same.

This stuff sure doesn't taste good, he thought. It probably was spoiled, because by the time the good food was cooked, he was sick and couldn't eat it.

★ ★ ★ ★ ★

"We think there is a Japanese outpost up on that hill, and we are supposed to go up and clear it out," the sergeant said to his group of men. "Let's go. It will soon be dark. Let's hope we can get it done before dark so we won't have to worry about the Japanese prowling around."

The group, with Desmond along as its medic, started up the trail. Before long the men saw four Japanese running across the hill. The four were soon eliminated, but the Americans had no idea where there might be more. And it was soon dark.

The sergeant told them, "Fellows, you had better bed down right along the trail. We hope there aren't any Japanese around, but be on your guard. There might be."

A little later when Desmond was sitting on the ground trying to get comfortable, he sensed something was near him.

"Halt!" he called out. He didn't have time to add, "Who goes there?" before something sharp hit his shoulder and then his head. Was it a bayonet? It almost felt like it.

"Meow! Meow!" The black cat, with its claws, nearly scared him to death for a second until he realized what it was—then he had a good chuckle.

DESMOND DOSS

★ ★ ★ ★ ★

The battle that took Guam away from the Japanese and put it back into American hands lasted until about the middle of August. Then for some time the soldiers stayed on the island to patrol it. It was sort of a vacation from war. The weather was beautiful and warm.

Desmond was happy for a few days when he could rest and sleep, write letters, and read the little Bible Dorothy had given him. He had a cold and felt tired most of the time. It was much later when he finally realized this was more than just a cold. He felt much better after a few days of rest. When the troop ship left Guam, he was ready to be a medic again.

The whole convoy left Guam on November 2. They headed south and heard that they were to go to New Caledonia for a period of rest and recreation until they were needed to fight in another area. The Pacific lived up to its name on that trip. The ocean was unbelievably calm. A few days later they crossed the equator into the southern hemisphere.

The convoy was traveling south, but one day the whole convoy turned around and headed northwest. General MacArthur had radioed that they were needed on Leyte, a large island in the Philippines. The troop ship landed on the east coast of Leyte and later went on around the island to the west coast.

"We're going up to the Ormoc River section in the northwest part of Leyte," the soldiers were told. The Japanese were well dug in there, and the seasoned soldiers knew they would be fighting a hard battle. They were right.

Whenever there was such a battle, the medics were working extra hard, caring for wounded men and taking them back to the aid station on stretchers.

★ ★ ★ ★ ★

One day B Company was moving to another bivouac area. As Desmond was walking along with the group, an infantry man approached him.

"Did you know that Glenn got hit?" he asked.

"No," answered Desmond. "Where is he?"

"Over on that hill right there," the soldier pointed.

Others had stopped when they heard the two talking. "I'm going to get him," Desmond said. "Will anyone go with me?"

"I will," said Herb Schechter. Desmond knew Schechter was a Jew who believed in predestination and that he would go places with Desmond when others wouldn't. Captain Vernon told five other soldiers to go with Doss and Schechter as a rear guard to help protect them in the exposed area to which they were going.

There were two wounded men on the hill—Glenn and the wounded soldier Glenn had gone to help. Desmond crouched low as he ran to the other soldier while Schechter ran to Glenn.

The young soldier had a nasty wound on his forehead, and blood had run down his face into his eyes, where it began to coagulate. Desmond got a bandage from his aid kit, moistened it with water from his canteen, and washed the blood from the soldier's face.

Suddenly the young man's face lit up with a smile, even in the dangerous place they found themselves in. "I thought I was blind," he said. Desmond remembered that smile all of his life and felt well repaid for the help he had given that soldier and others. The young soldier crawled back over a bank where other soldiers could help him get to the aid station.

Then Desmond turned his attention to Glenn. "How is he doing?" he called to Schechter.

"Hurt bad. Unconscious, but still alive," reported Schechter.

Evidently the Japanese were near and heard their voices. They started firing in the direction of the voices. Schechter jumped up and started running.

"Down, Schechter! Hit the dirt!" yelled Desmond.

Schechter went down so realistically that Desmond thought he had been hit. He crawled over to check him out and was more than glad to find he had not been hit.

"No more talking, Schechter," said Desmond. "Just whisper."

Now the question became what they could do for Glenn. He was a big man and quite heavy. The two medics took his poncho, spread it out on the ground and rolled Glenn onto it. Then they started to drag him back toward the aid station. They were in the open and had to pull him while stooping down as near to the ground as possible. At one place they pulled him over the body of a dead Japanese. They reached a brushy area. "I think we can stand up here," said Desmond.

He checked Glenn at this point. He was unconscious but still breathing!

DESMOND DOSS

The rear guard was there. Desmond borrowed a machete from one of the men and hacked down two bamboo poles. They tied the poncho onto the poles and started on, with two of the soldiers helping them. It was hot, and Desmond was getting very tired. But he was carrying his friend, so he kept pushing himself until they reached the bivouac area.

Desmond checked Glenn again. He didn't seem to be breathing! He checked his pulse. None! Clarence Glenn was dead!

Dr. Tann looked at Desmond and saw how tired and emotionally drained he was. He gave him a handful of pills and ordered him to take them and then go lie down. Those pills knocked him out, and he didn't wake up until the next day. When he did, he again remembered to thank God for His protection in a very dangerous situation.

Losing his best friend was a terrible shock to Desmond. From that time on he would try to do everything he could for the wounded soldiers, but he tried never to look at their faces—he didn't want to see another good friend dead.

Sometime later, Schechter and Doss were carrying a soldier on a stretcher. Just as they started up the bank of the river they had crossed, a sniper's bullet whistled past Desmond, hitting Schechter. Down he went.

"Come help me!" Desmond yelled to some soldiers on a litter jeep a short distance away. One soldier came to help Desmond take the man he and Schechter had been carrying to the jeep. Then they got another litter and came back to get Schechter. Just as they were putting him into the jeep, the Japanese started to spray them with machine gun bullets. The soldiers jumped into the jeep and took off. Desmond only had time to shove Schechter's litter a little farther onto the jeep and grab the back of the vehicle with his fingertips. He felt as though he flew most of the way back to the aid station, but he was thankful he even got there.

Herb Schechter never regained consciousness. Another good soldier and another good friend was gone. Desmond didn't dare let himself think about it.

★ ★ ★ ★ ★

When Desmond was with the fighting soldiers, he always tried to stay about two-thirds of the way back from the front of the group. That way he could more easily see and get to any wounded soldier. One day he was walking along, and before he realized what he was doing, he was right near the front of the line.

Just then a soldier next to him yelled and started clutching his foot, "Ow, that hurts!" he said.

Desmond stopped and examined the bullet hole in the man's foot. He bandaged it up. "Now, fellow, we had better give you a shot of morphine. It will help that foot feel better," suggested Desmond.

"No, I don't need any. It really doesn't hurt that bad," replied the soldier. He left to go back to the aid station as Desmond went on with the rest of his men. He really wanted to give the morphine to the soldier, but he never liked to go against a man's wishes. He knew that when the numbness wore off, that foot would begin to really hurt.

A little farther on, another soldier went down. He had been hit in the stomach, and Desmond could tell right away that he was badly hurt. The blast had ripped a big hole in his stomach, and his intestines were coming out. Desmond always believed in giving a man every chance he could, even when it looked hopeless. So he pushed the intestines back in and put a large battle dressing over the wound. The stretcher bearers took the soldier back to the aid station, but Desmond never thought he would reach there alive.

Next day he was at the aid station to pick up more bandages, so he asked about the two men.

"Oh," the doctor said. "The one with the hole in his foot? He died!"

"Really!" said Desmond. "He wasn't hurt that bad. What happened?"

"I don't really know. I guess it had to be shock. That can happen, you know," said the doctor.

"Well, what about the man with his intestines hanging out?" asked Desmond.

"They operated on him at the hospital, and I understand he is doing fine," replied the doctor.

Desmond could hardly believe it. But in later years he would meet this man at certain military functions. The man liked to say, "I have proof you took care of me," as he pointed to the scar across his middle.

★ ★ ★ ★ ★

Another day on Leyte, a soldier was wounded and lying at the edge of a rice paddy. As Desmond started to go to where he was, a couple of sergeants called to him, "You fool, take cover till things calm down. There is a sniper there, and we haven't got him. Do you have to go?"

"I think I should. If I wait, he might die before I get there," said Desmond.

He got to the man and found he was unconscious. He took care of his wounds and then called two litter bearers. They hurriedly rolled him onto the litter and took him to the aid station.

When he returned to where the sergeants were, they told him, "Doss, we expected to see you killed any second. We couldn't shoot the sniper without killing our own men, and he had his machine gun aimed right at you. Didn't you see him?"

"No," answered Desmond. And again, he thanked the Lord for His protection.

Three or four years later, a missionary in Japan was telling this story about Desmond. A man in the back of the room told one of the deacons, "That Japanese could very well have been me. I was there, and I remember having a soldier in my gun sight, but I couldn't pull the trigger." Later they wanted to question the man for more details, but he had disappeared.

★ ★ ★ ★ ★

On Leyte, Desmond had a weak spell. The soldiers were hiking through the jungle, knocking out Japanese resistance. They would hike for fifty minutes and then have a ten-minute break. Desmond found he couldn't keep up. He would catch up with the group just as the men were starting out again. This meant that most of the time he was hiking through the dangerous Japanese-infested jungle by himself. He could have easily been killed if the Lord had not protected him.

When the troops got to a rest area on the beach, the other soldiers rested and then played games, but not Desmond. He slept and slept and probably wouldn't even have eaten if Jim Dorris hadn't brought food to him. He felt better after the rest and was ready to go again. He knew God had cared for him.

At last, the island of Leyte was in American hands. Time for the 77th to move on. The American forces were closing in on the Japanese from every side. The island of Okinawa was only about 350 miles from Japan itself, and the Japanese were fighting hard there. So that is where the 77th Division was sent next.

Leyte had not been good to Desmond Doss. The loss of his two best friends was a tragedy he found hard to face. It was only as he prayed to his God and asked for strength that he felt able to bear the sadness.

CHAPTER FOURTEEN

OKINAWA

"Is that Okinawa? It doesn't look very big," remarked a soldier.

"No, I think that is just a small island near Okinawa. It is called Ie Shima. Shima means island. There is another island named Zamami Shima, I think," volunteered another soldier.

Yet another soldier had more information. "You know, I just heard that Ernie Pyle—he is that real nice war correspondent—was killed on Ie Shima just a day or two ago. It's too bad. He always stayed right with the men and told exactly what was happening to the soldiers on the battlefield."

For a few days the division stayed on board ship in the area.

But by April 20 the men were on the island of Okinawa itself. The 77th had many new recruits because so many of its soldiers had been wounded and killed on Guam and Leyte.

One thing made the soldiers sad when they landed on Okinawa. The Japanese had told the native Okinawans that Americans would treat them cruelly—rape their women and kill their children. They told the people to hide or even kill themselves to get away from these "terrible" Americans. Some mothers believed what they were told, and when the Americans landed on the island, they saw evidence that many mothers had slit their children's throats and then killed themselves. Others had thrown their children into the ocean from the high cliffs and then jumped in themselves. Hundreds lost their lives this way. The ones who didn't soon learned that the Americans were not as cruel as the Japanese had said they were.

Stretching across the island was a four-hundred-foot cliff, called the Maeda (Mi-e'-da) Escarpment, going almost straight up on the front side.

The top was about seventy-five to a hundred yards wide, then it sloped off down the back side.

Although the Americans didn't realize it until later, the Japanese were dug into the very center of that big hill. There were two- and three-story dugouts inside, connected by ladders from one story to another.

The 77th Division bivouacked in front of the four-hundred-foot cliff. Their job was to kill the Japanese on the top and back side of the escarpment. They began to realize what a job it was going to be.

As a medic, Desmond wasn't required to pull guard duty. But the soldiers had been fighting hard and losing a lot of sleep, so he volunteered for guard duty at times. One time, down near the bottom of the escarpment, he and another soldier were on guard. He took the first watch. After a couple of hours, he woke the other soldier—who immediately went back to sleep.

Then Desmond heard something! There was a big hole beside them; he could hear voices down the hole—and they weren't speaking English! There were grenades right beside him, and he knew that if he dropped a grenade down the hole, he would have some dead Japanese. Desmond felt this was the greatest temptation he ever had to destroy life. He believed that if a Japanese threw a grenade that landed in his lap, he would be justified in throwing it back before it exploded, but he felt it would cause confusion if he, a CO, dropped a grenade and killed someone. He poked the other soldier—he was snoring, and Desmond wondered if the Japanese could hear him. But the man immediately went back to sleep. So Desmond settled down as far away from the hole as he could and prayed for the rest of the night for the Lord's protection. His prayers were answered, and again he wasn't hurt.

From the bivouac area below the cliff, the soldiers could climb up about 360 feet, even though it was a hard climb because of the steepness and the roughness of the terrain. But the last 30 or 35 feet went almost straight up, even leaning out at the top about 5 feet from the vertical.

Later Lieutenant Gornto asked Desmond to help out. "Doss, could you and a couple of fellows get those navy cargo nets over there, and rig up a ladder for that last thirty feet or so? I think you can do it by splicing the nets together with two-by-fours."

"Yes, Sir. We'll try," said Desmond.

OKINAWA

They spliced the cargo nets together and tied them into the coral rock at the top edge of the escarpment. Other soldiers used rocks they found in the area to make a rock wall near the edge of the escarpment for the little protection it might give them.

"That's a good job, fellows," said the lieutenant. "It will sure help us to get up and down a lot easier—and safer, I hope."

On April 29, 1945, the real battle for the Maeda Escarpment began. The fighting took place on top of the escarpment after the soldiers got to the top. One big problem they found was that the Japanese had been there for so long that they had been able to dig trenches and foxholes that the Americans couldn't even tell were trenches or foxholes. The area looked like natural terrain, but unseen guns were sticking out to shoot the unsuspecting Americans.

Henry D. Lopez, in his book *From Jackson to Japan,* says, "Japanese defenses on Okinawa were the most rugged and impregnable ever assaulted. . . . The terrain of Okinawa with its countless knolls, ridges, and promontories of coral-limestone rock . . . lent itself most favorably to the conduct of a determined defense."

★ ★ ★ ★ ★

Miracle day

"OK, fellows, we're going up on top again today. Those cargo nets are up, so we can get on top more easily. You have plenty of ammunition. Do your best, men." Lieutenant Gornto was giving last minute instructions.

Desmond went over to where Gornto was. "Lieutenant," he said, "I believe prayer is the best life saver there is. The men should really pray before they go up."

"Fellows," called Gornto, "come over here and gather around. Doss wants to pray for us."

That wasn't what Desmond had in mind! He had felt that the men should be reminded to pray for themselves before going up the cargo net because no one knew whether he would survive this battle. But when Lieutenant Gornto put it that way, Desmond did pray. "Dear Lord," he said when the men had gathered around, "bless us today. Be with the lieutenant and help him to give the right orders, for our lives are in his hands. Help each one of us to use safety precautions so that we all might come back alive. And, Lord, help all of us to make our peace with Thee before we go up the net. Thank You. Amen."

With that, they all started up the cliff and the cargo net. They reached the top and almost immediately got pinned down, unable to move on. Company A was fighting to their left and was hitting fierce opposition. The first five men in Company A who reached the top were killed. A message came by radio from headquarters asking how many of the Company B men had been killed or wounded.

Desmond reported none so far. So the orders were given that Company B should take the whole hilltop by itself because Company A was pretty well shot up. Uncle Sam has to sacrifice lives at times to gain important objectives, and the Maeda Escarpment was an important objective.

So Company B started across the top of the escarpment. The men knocked out eight or nine Japanese pillboxes. The miracle of the story was that not one man in Company B was killed, and only one man was injured—by a rock that hit his hand.

It was such an outstanding event that headquarters soon heard about it, and the news went back even to the States.

"How did you ever do it?" was the question asked.

The men of Company B answered, "It was because of Doss's prayer."

The next day a member of the Signal Corp arrived at the Company B area. "We've heard about the good job you guys did yesterday. Can I get a picture?"

"Yes," said Lieutenant Gornto. "Doss, go up on the escarpment and let him take your picture."

Desmond said to the Signal Corp man, "Come on up with me."

"I don't believe I will. I haven't lost anything up there and don't intend to."

★ ★ ★ ★ ★

Medal of Honor day

It was time to go up on the escarpment again. Although in the heat of battle, it isn't always possible to remember which day is which, it is believed from other sources that this was on Sabbath, May 5.

Desmond was reading his Bible when Captain Vernon approached him and said, "Doss, would you mind going up on the escarpment today? You know, you are the only medic we have left, and we really need you."

"Yes, Captain. I'll go up. But do you suppose I could take time to finish my private devotions?" asked Desmond.

"OK, we'll wait for you," the captain replied.

Desmond was studying his Sabbath School lesson. The topic was about following Jesus. He finished and bowed his head in prayer. Later, he figured he was ready to join the group about ten minutes after Captain Vernon had asked him to go up on the escarpment. Some told him afterward that it was a half hour. But none of the men were eager to go up and fight, so they were glad for the delay.

The soldiers actually thought the hardest battle had already been fought and that this day would be just a mop-up job. Desmond again mentioned praying, but Captain Vernon said, "Sorry, Doss, we've already started to push off." So nothing more was said about prayer.

The 155 men left in Company B went up the escarpment. Right away they faced the hell of war. Everything seemed to go wrong. One Japanese position the group could not seem to rout. The Americans heaved satchel charges (bags of TNT) and other high explosives into the Japanese position, but the enemy pulled out the fuses before they exploded. Finally, several of the men grabbed five-gallon cans of gasoline and heaved them over into the Japanese foxholes. Then Lieutenant Phillips threw in a white phosphorus grenade.

The result was more than they had anticipated. There was a terrific explosion in the foxhole itself, but an even greater explosion further down in the hill. Evidently, not only did all of the high explosives the men had thrown into the foxhole explode when the gasoline ignited, but also an ammunition dump deeper in the hillside.

What happened next was totally unexpected. From all directions, Japanese emerged from other foxholes and trenches; they probably figured it was now or never. There were so many Japanese and they fought so hard, it would have been suicide for the Americans to stay on top of the escarpment. The soldiers were ordered to retreat. It was supposed to be an orderly retreat, but it ended in panic.

Desmond was up on top with his men—until they all left. But what about the wounded men who were scattered around on the top of the escarpment? He couldn't go off and leave them. He knew many of them had families at home.

He started for the nearest soldier; he was badly hurt. Desmond dragged him over to the edge of the escarpment and looked around to see what he had to use. There was a litter and the one rope they had used for hauling up supplies. He rolled the wounded soldier onto the litter and tied him on as well as he could. Then he dropped him over the edge as he hung on to the rope. Part way down, he thought he was going to lose the man, but the rope held, and the litter landed safely thirty-five feet below at the bottom of the cargo net.

Some of the soldiers had dropped to the ground at the bottom of the cargo net to rest for a minute before proceeding on down the cliff. "What on earth is going on?" they wondered as they noticed the litter coming down.

"Take him to the aid station pronto," yelled Desmond from up on top. "He's hurt bad."

As a couple of fellows started on down the cliff with the wounded man, Desmond pulled the rope back up. It had taken a long time to lower that man. Then Desmond remembered the bowline knot with the two loops that he had tied back during training at Elkins, West Virginia. He believes today that God brought it to his mind. He quickly tied this knot, brought another wounded man over to the edge of the cliff and slid the two loops onto his legs. Then he doubled the rope again and tied it around the man's chest. Then he let him gently over the edge. The Lord even provided a tree stump at that spot on top of the hill. Desmond wound the rope around the stump and let the rope play out gradually. That took the load off him as he let the man down. All the time he kept praying, "Lord, help me get one more."

Why the Japanese didn't come over to the part of the escarpment where the wounded Americans were and finish them all off, Desmond didn't know. His only explanation was that God took care of him and his men. Later he had time to thank God. He didn't feel he would be killed because he remembered that he had never dishonored his parents, and the fifth commandment says if you honor your parents, your days will be long on the land which the Lord your God gives you. He didn't feel that would keep him from being wounded, but he felt it would be worth it to get wounded if he could save his men.

It took Desmond about five hours, but he rescued all of the wounded soldiers. It was a tired, thankful, blood-soaked soldier who finally came down the Maeda Escarpment that day. And, unbelievably, he was not wounded!

The members of Company B who had witnessed this medic, this conscientious objector soldier, doing what he did were astonished; it wasn't long before the rest of the company heard about it, too. Then others.

When he arrived back at the bivouac area, he heard welcome words. "Doss, those fatigues are blood-soaked. Besides, you're covered with flies, and we don't have any fly spray. We're going to have to find you some different fatigues." Before long he was dressed in a clean uniform. He decided to go off to a quiet place somewhere and read his Bible. He certainly had something special to thank his God for this time!

While he was gone, General A. D. Bruce from the 77th Division headquarters arrived at the camp. He had heard of Desmond's feat and wanted to shake his hand. He also suggested that he should receive the Congressional Medal of Honor and asked those who could start the process to get it going. Desmond learned of this later because he was not there to shake the general's hand. He wished he had been.

How many men had Desmond let down from the escarpment? The top brass said, "Let's see. We had 155 men go up, and only 55 men got down the hill on their own. So you must have saved a hundred men."

"That couldn't be," said Desmond, modestly. "It couldn't have been more than fifty. I wouldn't have had time to save a hundred men."

So they compromised at seventy-five, and that is the number on Desmond's Congressional Medal of Honor citation.

★ ★ ★ ★ ★

Two weeks later there were still places where the Japanese were fighting hard. It was decided to try Japanese tactics—they came out of hiding early in the morning to find sleeping Americans and kill them. Why shouldn't the Americans do the same?

The officers decided to try it. One very dark night the American soldiers marched out of their bivouac area. Desmond plastered a piece of adhesive tape on the back of each man's pack so they could follow each other from the faint glow it made. But it was so dark even that didn't help. They finally got near the area where they were to be next morning. Desmond and three others found a hole and crawled in.

DESMOND DOSS

They saw it coming! A grenade! The other three managed to crawl out, but Desmond was too far back in the hole. The grenade landed at his feet. Almost without thinking he put his heavy army boot on top of the grenade. BOOM!! He felt himself flying into the air, and he saw stars that weren't there. When he was on the ground again, he felt his leg. It was still there! But it was bleeding badly. He bandaged the leg as best he could.

He had to get out of the area because it was Japanese territory, so he and another soldier started crawling over the hill into American territory. They found a hole there. Because the other soldier was wounded in his shoulder, Desmond borrowed his shovel to dig the hole a little wider. Then they crawled in to spend the rest of the night. Desmond knew he was losing a lot of blood. He felt woozy and lay with his head down the hill. When it began to get light, the two men looked around a little. They saw that when Desmond had been shoveling the night before to widen the hole, he had come within inches of hitting an unexploded artillery shell. If he had hit it, there wouldn't have been a grease spot left, as the saying goes.

Again God had cared for Desmond.

Soon after daybreak, the litter bearers came to pick up the wounded. They loaded Desmond on the litter and started for the aid station. On the way, they found a soldier who had been wounded in the head when the Japanese opened fire. But they had only one litter and not enough men to carry two soldiers. Desmond rolled off the litter and told them to take the man who had the head wound.

"We don't want to do that, Doss," they said. But Desmond insisted. "I've been out here for five hours, and I'll be OK for a while yet. Take him."

"Well, OK, Doss, but we'll be back shortly."

While they were gone, Brooks, a friend from Dorothy's home town of Richmond, Virginia, came by. He had been slightly wounded.

"Doss, what happened to you? Oh, I see. If you lean on me, do you suppose we could manage to get to the aid station on our own? Come on, let's try it," suggested Brooks.

They started out, but hadn't gone far when a Japanese sniper shot Desmond, hitting him in the arm. The bullet went into his wrist, came out below his elbow, went back in above his elbow, and lodged in his upper arm, shattering bones and nerves. If the bullet hadn't hit Desmond's arm, it probably would have gone through Brooks's neck, possibly killing him.

"Brooks, give me your gun," Desmond said. Brooks wondered why this man who had never carried a gun wanted one all of a sudden. But Desmond knew. He put it against his useless arm and asked Brooks to wrap his field jacket around both his arm and his body. It made a splint for the arm. They went on toward the aid station, but Desmond had lost so much blood he passed out. Brooks ran to the aid station and got the litter bearers there to go out and pick up Desmond. The aid station they arrived at was not the First Battalion aid station. That caused an interesting happening in Lynchburg, Virginia.

When the original litter bearers from the First Battalion came back to get Desmond, he was gone. So they reported him killed in action, and that report went back to Lynchburg, where it was printed in the newspaper. But while Desmond was in the hospital after surgery on his leg and arm, he asked a nurse to help him finish his letter to his folks, which he sent home.

The day after the newspaper came out with the story that Desmond Doss had been killed in action, Mother Doss went to work as usual at the shoe factory. Her fellow workers were shocked. "Mrs. Doss, how can you come to work when your boy was killed?"

"But he wasn't killed! He was wounded and is in the hospital, but he will be OK eventually. You see, we got a letter from him just yesterday." The next day the paper printed a retraction.

When Desmond arrived at the field hospital, the doctor looked at his wounded arm and leg, and said, "Doss, we are marking you for stateside as soon as we get you fixed up a little." Desmond decided that was one nice thing about being wounded.

Surgery for Desmond meant taking out seventeen pieces of shrapnel from his wounded leg and setting his wounded arm, putting it in a heavy cast. After surgery he was put on a hospital ship, heading east this time. It was about that time that he noticed his little Bible was missing! He must have dropped it out on the battlefield. He sent a message back to his fellow soldiers, asking them to keep an eye open for it. His friends fanned out across the area, and it was found and returned to Desmond. He treasured that Bible.

DESMOND DOSS

The hospital ship took him to Guam, and a plane flew him on to Hawaii.

"My arm really hurts, and besides, it smells terrible," Desmond told the corpsman who was helping him.

"We'll have the doctor take a look," the soldier replied.

The doctor had to cut out a piece of the cast to get to the arm. He found the gauze bandage was wrapped through the bones, and the arm was infected. When he saw the condition of Desmond's arm, he had a few well-chosen swear words to say about a certain doctor in Okinawa. "If that man were a veterinarian, I wouldn't even take my dog to him!" he exploded.

"Doctor, is there anything you can do to make this cast more comfortable? It's awfully heavy, and it doesn't let me stand up straight," said Desmond as the doctor worked on his arm.

"Well, it is getting in kind of bad shape. If it gets in a little worse shape, we might need to change it."

So Desmond saw to it that the cast did get in worse shape in a very short time. As a result, the old heavy cast was removed and a new type of splint was put on his arm. It was made of metal strips and covered with muslin and called an "airplane splint."

When the doctor finished with Desmond's arm, it felt much better—and it didn't stink!

Then he continued his journey across the Pacific toward home.

CHAPTER FIFTEEN

HOME AGAIN

"Sweetheart, I'm home. Well, not home yet, but home in the U.S. I'm in Seattle. I don't know yet how soon I'll be in Virginia, but I'll be there as soon as I can," said Desmond over the phone.

When he arrived in Seattle, Desmond was told he could have one free phone call. His would be to Dorothy, of course, but where was she? Her letters to him hadn't reached him since he was wounded. He knew she had been teaching school in Norfolk, but this was summertime. When he called Richmond, Mother Schutte said Dorothy was at Washington Missionary College taking school work for the summer. So he called Washington.

Desmond's phone call was what Dorothy had been waiting to hear. What a joy to hear his voice. He had written to her, telling about what had happened to him, but that wasn't like hearing his welcome voice.

"Hi, honey. I love you, and it is so good to actually hear your voice. Desmond, I want to come to Seattle to see you. Can I?" asked Dorothy.

"Sweetheart, I don't even know how long I will be here. I hear they will be sending me somewhere near home. So you had better wait till I get back there," answered Desmond.

In a few days he was in Asheville, North Carolina, at the Swannenoa Hospital. His parents came to see him there. It was wonderful to see them, but he still hadn't seen Dorothy. They wanted to see each other so much. He talked to her on the phone again.

"Desmond, I want to come to Asheville. I still have about two weeks of summer school, but I'll just quit," Dorothy said.

DESMOND DOSS

"Honey, you know I want to see you, but I don't think you should give up your whole summer's work. Stay there and finish. The time will go fast," Desmond suggested. So it was decided that would be best. But Dorothy did manage to take her final tests a few days early.

But "all things come to him who waits." Dorothy went home to Richmond, and Desmond boarded the bus for Richmond.

Mother Schutte drove Dorothy to the bus station, and at last Desmond had his Dorothy in his arms—at least in his one good arm. It was wonderful to be together again!

Desmond still had the bullet in his upper arm, and he was transferred to Woodrow Wilson Hospital near Waynesboro, Virginia, where they took it out. It wasn't long before the cast was gone also. He began to feel like a human being again.

One day the hospital commander stopped by his room.

"Are you ready to go to Washington?" he asked.

"What do you mean by that?" Desmond asked in turn.

"We're going to take you to Washington to get that Congressional Medal of Honor. We'll even take you there in my own staff car. Can your wife go with you? What about your parents? We hope they can be there, too."

What a pleasant surprise, and what a pleasant time they had in Washington. The story of this Seventh-day Adventist soldier who was going to receive the Congressional Medal of Honor had been told over and over in Seventh-day Adventist churches everywhere. His picture and his story were even published in the *Review and Herald,* the official church publication. Several of the officers of the General Conference of Seventh-day Adventists in Washington, D.C., attended the ceremonies on the White House lawn on October 12, 1945, when President Harry S. Truman placed the blue ribbon with the medal attached around Desmond's neck. His "Congressional Medal of Honor Citation" was read at the ceremony. A copy of the citation is on the page following the title page in this book.

When he left Washington, he asked and received permission to take his long-overdue furlough in Richmond, Virginia. There was really no reason for him to return to Woodrow Wilson Hospital, so he went to the army hospital in Richmond and asked about being transferred to Richmond. "Just check in sick here. Then you won't have to go back there at all," they told him.

"I can't do that. I'm not sick, and it wouldn't be honest," said Desmond. He went back to Woodrow Wilson Hospital and was transferred later. Now he was a patient at the army hospital in Richmond, but was working in the hydrotherapy department and liking it. But he found that although he felt all right in the morning, by noon he was so tired he could hardly keep going.

"Desmond Doss, can you come to our church—or to our camp meeting or to our youth rally—and tell your experiences?" That question came to him over and over, and he found himself "on the road," especially on weekends.

One week he was supposed to go to California for a weekend youth rally, but he felt so tired and worn out and seemed to have a hacking cough all the time. He went to see the army doctor.

"Doc, I have a cough I can't seem to get over, and I'm tired all the time," Desmond told him.

"What have you been doing to make you tired?"

"Traveling all over the country, speaking on weekends." He told the doctor about his Medal of Honor, and why he was traveling. "I'm supposed to go to California this weekend and I don't feel up to it."

"Seems like you need a doctor's orders to stay home. You had better not go this weekend. Stay home and rest," the doctor said. So Desmond canceled the appointment. The next week he developed a sharp pain in his chest, so he went to the doctor again. "I think we had better take a chest X-ray and see what is going on," the doctor said. The X-ray was taken, and Desmond waited for the report.

"Doss, you will need some more X-rays," the doctor told him. When the doctor had those results in his hands, he said, "Doss, we're going to transfer you to another ward. You will have to stay here in the hospital." Actually he was transferred to a private room in another ward.

What was this all about anyway? Desmond finally got the answer to his questions—he had tuberculosis (TB)! And he was going to have to stay in the hospital. He called Dorothy. "Sweetheart, I'm here at the hospital, and they won't let me come home. I've just found out I have TB." He was very upset.

"Oh, no, Desmond! Just when we were ready to settle down and live a regular life. And with me pregnant!" Desmond could only say, "I'm sorry, sweetheart."

One thing he was upset about was that Dorothy could come to see him only during visiting hours, and since she was teaching, she couldn't get there during visiting hours. He explained that to the doctor, and the doctor said, "Don't you worry about that. I'll make arrangements so that she can come to see you anytime she wants to."

Desmond remembered the times when he was in the Pacific and got a cold he couldn't shake and when he was too tired to keep up with his buddies. He told the doctor about those times. "Was I getting TB then?" he asked.

"You probably were," answered the doctor.

For the next five and a half years, Desmond spent most of his time in VA hospitals. It would take a whole book just to tell all the things that happened to him during that time, but a few interesting things can be told.

He was first sent to Fitzsimmons Hospital in Colorado because that facility had a good record for treating TB. But he was so lonesome for Dorothy and so worried about her. She was teaching school again, and he knew she would stay up half the night to get things perfect for the next day. And she was pregnant. His worries made his health go downhill.

Dr. Dart, an Adventist physician at the hospital, had a cousin, Archa Dart, who was in educational work and who was Dorothy's supervisor. So Dr. Dart wrote to Supervisor Dart and told him, "Desmond needs Dorothy more than you do." That was how Dorothy happened to come to Colorado. And Desmond did get better.

★ ★ ★ ★ ★

Many of the Adventist people in the area of Asheville, North Carolina, where Desmond was for some time, came to visit him. Two came one Sabbath afternoon. "Anything we can do for you or get for you?" they asked.

"I surely wish I could get some wire recordings (the forerunner of cassette tapes) and something to play them on. It would help pass the time and give me something to listen to on Sabbath. I can't go to church, you know."

"I think I have a recorder at home I could let you use," one of them said. So he brought it to Desmond with many recordings to play. Now Desmond enjoyed listening to recordings and sharing the music with others at times.

★ ★ ★ ★ ★

Another time Sug came to see him. Sug was the matron at the institution. She was "Sug" to all the patients, and they were all "Sug" to her.

"Sug, do you really want us to get well?" asked Desmond.

"Of course, Sug. Why?" she asked.

"Well, the patients here are given all the free cigarettes they can smoke. They aren't good for you, you know. But they want to cut down on the amount of milk we can have. How come?"

"Sug," she said, "you'll get your milk."

★ ★ ★ ★ ★

Desmond had many X-rays, bronchoscopes, and other treatments. The TB was in both lungs, but his left lung was worse than the right one. The bronchoscope was to stretch his bronchial tubes so that he could breath better. The doctor gave him a bronchoscope about every two weeks. He would spit up blood for a week and just begin to feel better when the whole thing was repeated.

One day Desmond was taken to the lab for another blood test. (He wondered if he would have any blood left.) After the test, he was taken to the surgery department. "What is this all about?" he asked.

"Orders," said the orderly, and he would say nothing more.

When a doctor came to the waiting room a little later, he remarked, "I suppose you know why you are here."

"No, I don't know. That's what I'm trying to find out," said Desmond.

"I'll talk to you in a minute." When he came out again he showed Desmond his X-rays and explained to him the necessity of removing his left lung.

"Just what would be my chances of survival if I didn't have the operation?" Desmond asked.

"None," said the doctor.

"What are the chances with the surgery?"

"Fifty-fifty."

"Doc, I'm a vegetarian," said Desmond, thinking it might help him have a better chance.

"Doss, you'll never pull through this surgery without having a very high protein diet. The only way you can get enough protein is to eat meat.

"Doctor, I will go ahead with the surgery, but I won't eat the meat. I do have lots of milk, eggs, and cottage cheese, and I buy my own soybeans and they give me half a can a day. Shouldn't that be enough?"

"I don't know," said the doctor, "but if you insist on doing it that way, we'll have to see how it works out."

Pretty discouraging! Desmond thought. Out loud he asked, "When do I have the surgery?"

A date was set about two weeks later. In the meantime, Dorothy called friends and interested people all over the United States and asked them to remember Desmond in prayer. Elder Roach, a Seventh-day Adventist minister, was contacted, and he promised to come in to pray with Desmond on the morning of surgery.

Elder Roach came, also Dorothy, and Desmond's parents. But the orderly came to get him an hour earlier than he was supposed to. So when they all arrived, the nurses were already getting Desmond ready for surgery. He received word that they were there, and he insisted that he wanted to have prayer before going into surgery.

So they wheeled him back out to where Dorothy, his parents, and Elder Roach were. They gathered round while Elder Roach prayed for Desmond.

After that, Desmond felt completely at ease as they again wheeled him into surgery. Desmond was sure that God knew all about him and that He would care for him and do what was best for him.

Later, after the surgery, Desmond was told that he had come through the operation better than any of the other patients. Also that his spine was the straightest of any of their surgical patients. Anyone who has seen Desmond will testify to that.

Again he knew that God had cared for him.

HOME AGAIN

About this time, doctors were beginning to use antibiotics for many diseases—one of them being TB. They used the anitbiotics for Desmond. The only problem was their use was still in the experimental stage, and no one knew exactly how much to give. Desmond remembers one kind of medicine he had to take by mouth and how it tasted terrible and made him sick! The other medicine was administered by a hypodermic needle, and he got so sore he could hardly sit down. But the antibiotics did help him, and soon his tests were all running negative.

"Doctor, my ears constantly ring. How come?" he asked one day.

"Probably a little reaction to the antibiotics. It should clear up soon," the doctor answered.

But it didn't. Not only that—Desmond was finding it harder and harder to hear. For approximately the next twenty-five years, Desmond became more and more deaf. At first, hearing aids helped, but eventually, he couldn't make out what people were saying, even when wearing his hearing aids. Doctors have told him his hearing loss was no doubt due to the antibiotics he took in the experimental stage when doctors didn't really know how much to give him.

CHAPTER SIXTEEN

CAMP DOSS

"I know we've had many Medical Cadet Corps training courses to help our Adventist boys who are in line for the draft, but how would it be if we opened up a national camp where the boys could come and get a good training course that would help them? You know, too, that there are a lot of boys who don't live near places where the MCC classes are taught," said Colonel Everett Dick, one of the officers of the Seventh-day Adventist National Service Organization, approaching Carlyle B. Haynes, his boss, with his idea.

"That sounds like a good idea," answered Haynes. "And I think I know a place where we could have it. The Michigan Conference would let us use its camp meeting site near Grand Ledge, I think.

"You know, I was the president of that conference at one time."

Another thing they discussed was what name they would give to the camp. "Remember that young fellow who got the Medal of Honor? His name is Desmond Doss. Why don't we call the camp, Camp Desmond Doss?" Haynes suggested. That was agreeable to all concerned.

The camp was established in Michigan as they hoped, and it was named Camp Desmond Doss. Desmond spent time at the camp at various times, helping the leaders and talking to the fellows who registered for the course and encouraging them.

Because of the terrible pressure Dorothy had been under during the time Desmond was being treated for TB—and some other stressful things that came up—she had a nervous breakdown. She felt she would never be able to do anything worthwhile again or even keep house.

On the advice of a person who had been in the same condition, Desmond took Dorothy to a medical center at Wildwood, Georgia, where the staff used nourishing food, exercise, and rest to help people get over such things. Dorothy was admitted as a patient and was there for more than a year. During that time, Desmond's parents and his sister Audrey took care of Tommy, Desmond and Dorothy's new baby, while Desmond was at work. Desmond would drive the 250 miles to see Dorothy almost every weekend.

One weekend, Dorothy and others suggested that he take a leave of absence from his work and come stay at Wildwood. He could work on maintenance there and not have to travel back and forth. He decided to do that.

One day Roy Cooper, one of the other workers at Wildwood, suggested, "Desmond, a lady, Mrs. Terry, is starting a school up on Lookout Mountain. Would you like to go up there with some of the rest of us and help build some buildings?"

"I believe I would like to do that. I'll pray about it, too," he answered. As he prayed he felt the Lord would want him to do that. So Desmond took Tommy and went to Lookout Mountain, about twenty miles from Wildwood. Edith, Roy's wife, helped him care for Tommy. Again he felt God was providing for his needs.

Desmond found a five-acre piece of property on the mountain with a small, old three-room cabin on it. It really was old. Pans were put around to catch the roof-leaks when it rained, and when the wind blew, the linoleum bounced up and down on the floor. He cashed in his army insurance policy and bought it in 1955. Dorothy was getting better by now, but she wasn't happy that Desmond bought the property because she still felt she could never keep house again. How wrong she was. Later on she not only kept house but finished a nursing course and got her R.N. degree and even a B.S. in nursing.

Desmond built on other rooms all around the original three rooms until he had quite a large home, but the original three rooms are still a part of the house. Desmond and Dorothy settled down in the little house that soon became home to them, and they thanked the Lord for it.

DESMOND DOSS

"Hello, Desmond. This is Clark Smith." Desmond wondered why Clark Smith, one of the officers of the National Service Organization, was calling him. "We have a chance to make a film to help our soldiers, and we want to tell your story. But we thought it would be wonderful if you could go to California and talk for the film. It sure would improve the quality of it."

"Clark, I don't know. I've been gone so much speaking at different places, and I'm having trouble with my well and need to work on it. Besides, you know that Josephine Cunnington Edwards is writing my story, and I need to be here to answer any questions she might have."

"Well, Desmond, we just can't let this opportunity pass. Did I tell you a man was paying for the whole thing—that doesn't happen very often. Tell you what. Give me Mrs. Edward's phone number, and I'll call her and see if it is OK with her to have you gone for a few days. We really want you. How about it?" said Clark.

Desmond turned from the phone and briefly explained the situation to Dorothy.

"I think you should go, Desmond," was her advice.

So Desmond found himself on the way to California, on a train this time instead of a plane. Clark Smith had arranged for the ticket and told him, because the program had to be done at a certain time, that he must let them know right away if he missed a train connection. He almost did one time!

Clark Smith and Des Cummings, president of the Southeastern California Conference, met him at the train. When they went to check his baggage—no baggage! It hadn't kept up with him, and the meeting was to be held that evening.

"That's OK," said Clark. "We'll visit some army surplus places and see what we can find."

They spent a lot of time looking for a good uniform, but they did take time to go to a cafeteria for dinner. Clark and Des seemed to want to make sure Desmond had plenty to eat, so they kept putting food on his tray.

He protested, "Hey, you guys. I'll never be able to eat all of that."

"Just eat what you can," they assured him. He didn't realize then that they were doing everything they could to kill time.

Soon it was time for them to go to the studio for the program. A man had picked them up from the hotel where they had registered Desmond. He had changed into the uniform they had bought that day. They all agreed he looked nice.

When they got to the studio, the driver drove up to a gate and the gatekeeper opened it immediately. Desmond seemed a little surprised. The driver remarked, "Don't worry about that. I just work here."

Desmond was taken into a studio room in the back of the building, but soon he was at the podium, talking to the soldiers by film. He had no sooner started talking than a man came in and interrupted him. *What is this all about?* Desmond wondered. *Why is he interrupting me when I am trying to talk?* Also Desmond had never seen a person "fixed up" for TV before, and he thought the man looked sort of clownish.

The man was very polite. "Desmond Doss, from Rising Fawn, Georgia, and the recipient of the Congressional Medal of Honor, you are now on *This Is Your Life!* I'm Ralph Edwards."

Desmond couldn't believe what he heard. But he soon found himself on a platform with hundreds of people in the audience. Ralph Edwards was giving the people a brief history of his military career and what he had done to receive the Medal of Honor.

This interview program had brought in many friends and associates to surprise the honored guest. Three of Desmond's army friends were there, Major Cooney, O. C. Brister, and Fred Carr. Audrey Doss-Millner, his sister, and Harold, his brother, were there. Also his parents, Thomas and Bertha Doss. And at last, but not least, Dorothy and his son Tommy were there. What a surprise! It was also nerve-wracking! One time Desmond told Ralph Edwards, "This is worse than combat."

He received many lovely gifts—a table saw, a small garden tractor with attachments, an Edsel station wagon, and even money with which to buy some more land to add to the five acres he had bought on Lookout Mountain. He and all of his relatives and friends were treated to a lovely dinner in the hotel that evening.

Desmond began to realize why some recent events had happened as they did. The long train trip, he now knew, gave his relatives, especially Dorothy and Tommy, the chance to fly out to California. He knew now why Dorothy had encouraged him to go to California—she knew about *This Is Your Life*. He recognized why Clark Smith had called and asked him to come, and he also could see why he was told there wasn't time to go to the Voice of Prophecy (his favorite religious radio program) offices in Glendale. Someone there would have let the cat out of the bag, and the whole thing had to be kept secret from Desmond or the program would not have been aired. Ralph Edwards would have substituted another program.

He also learned that Josephine Cunnington Edwards, who was writing a book about him, had been asking him for information that she was giving to Ralph Edwards for the program. She was a distant relative of Ralph's and a very popular Adventist writer; she was the one who had suggested his name to Ralph Edwards. Because her husband died shortly after this, she didn't feel up to finishing the book, so the project was given to another writer, Booten Herndon. He wrote the book, *The Unlikeliest Hero*.

One other thing needs to be added. Desmond and Dorothy liked to pay tithe on even the gifts they received. They kept track of the amount owed, but they were so hard up they hadn't paid it. But Desmond remembered the experiences his mother had when she paid her tithe. So they decided to give God the tithe even though it left very little for them to use for expenses. Only a month afterwards, Desmond was on *This Is Your Life*. That gave them a boost, and from then on their finances were much better. Desmond knew that God had cared for him and blessed him again.

★ ★ ★ ★ ★

About this time Desmond realized that, because of his TB experience and losing a lung, he could not keep up with an eight-hour work day. He checked with several doctors and the Veterans Administration, and eventually he was put on permanent disability.

So for the next fifteen years, approximately, Desmond worked on his five acres, which had become thirteen acres because of the additional land he had bought with the money from *This Is Your Life*. This additional land was mostly woods, with many delicate wildflowers and pretty green moss on it. One winter there was a terrible ice storm, and many trees fell. He cleaned up the debris, and the county came in and put in a dam, so now there is a lovely little lake on the property.

He also spent many weekends and even weeks at times going on speaking engagements. His hearing was not good, but he managed. Those who asked him to come and speak would pay his traveling expenses, but Desmond never charged for the talk itself—he wanted to do that as an appreciation to the Lord for His care. However, he would tell about building the little church on Lookout Mountain, and many times an offering was taken for that. With the offering Desmond would buy needed materials for the church, and when he was at home, he spent many hours working on the building. Today there is a beautiful little Adventist church on Lookout Mountain.

CHAPTER SEVENTEEN

DEAFNESS AND A COCHLEAR IMPLANT

I guess I'd better fix that door lock on the bedroom door, thought Desmond. He got out the needed tools and started the job. This was in 1976. Dorothy was a good nurse by now, and she was working that day, but she would be home soon.

Suddenly Desmond felt very dizzy. "I wonder what is the matter with me," he muttered to himself. "I guess I'll lie down for a few minutes."

In the meantime Dorothy came home from work to find some people in her front yard. "We came to see Desmond," they said. "We know he is in there, but he doesn't answer the door."

"I'll go see what the problem is," she said. So she went into the house and found Desmond lying on the couch.

"What's the matter, Honey?" she asked. No answer, but he looked at her with a puzzled expression on his face.

"Desmond, can't you hear me?" She knew Desmond was deaf. She had lived with his deafness for years. But he could usually hear something and would answer her. This time he didn't answer.

He looked at her with that puzzled expression again. He thought she had lost her voice. Then he shook his head.

Both of them suddenly realized he was totally deaf; he could hear nothing! It was afternoon by this time, and Desmond decided to go to the VA hospital in Atlanta right away to see if he could get help there. On the way he stopped at the conference office in Calhoun, Georgia, to leave his church treasurer's report, which he had just finished. He also told the people there that he was totally deaf and asked them to pray for him.

DEAFNESS AND A COCHLEAR IMPLANT

Then he went on to Atlanta.

"We'll check you into a hotel room for the night and see you in the morning," the people told him at the VA hospital.

"I'm not going to do that," said Desmond. "I can't hear a thing, and I need to see a doctor now."

Bess, one of the volunteer workers, took him under her wing and made sure he had a hospital bed and that the doctor would see him that evening.

They checked him over, decided it was nerve deafness, and put him on IVs, trying to save what nerves they could. Nothing seemed to help permanently, and he went home to an almost silent world. He could hear a little of what sounded like noise, but he could not tell what the noise was.

For the next twelve years that was the way it was. Dorothy had to write out any information he received, at home or at church or anywhere else.

"Honey, I'm your hearing ear dog," Dorothy told him.

Quite a few things he had to give up doing—things at church, for instance. He was the first elder at his church, and he was the church treasurer. With no hearing he couldn't manage to do those jobs anymore.

"How about it, can you keep up with being the chief of Walker County rescue work, Desmond?" his fellow rescue workers asked. That was a good question. Desmond had been chief of the county rescue work for years, and had built up the work with good equipment and good workers.

Any problems in caves, of which there were a number in the area, Desmond was always there. He wouldn't ask any of the other fellows to do what he wasn't willing to do himself. One time the rescue crew had to rescue some fellows in a cave. They did bring them out, but two of them died from the effects of the gases in the cave. Those same gases made it extra hard for Desmond to breathe. He was taken to the hospital and nearly lost his life with pneumonia. This was yet another time God took care of him.

"No, I won't be able to be chief of rescue without being able to hear. I guess I will have to quit and let you fellows take it over," he answered their question. It was hard to give up.

Years went by. Probably about the middle of the 1980s, Desmond began to hear about something called a cochlear implant. It was supposed to help those who were totally deaf.

DESMOND DOSS

"Sweetheart, please call and ask the VA if they know anything about this new thing called a cochlear implant," Desmond suggested to Dorothy.

Dorothy called. Yes, they knew something about it, but not very much yet. Yes, they would keep Desmond in mind and let him know of any developments.

Some weeks later the VA called Desmond to tell him it was going to send him to the VA hospital at West Haven, Connecticut, where doctors were beginning to give the cochlear implant to patients if they thought they were good candidates. That was one time when Desmond went by himself. He missed Dorothy being with him as she usually was, but she couldn't go. However, the VA typed out notes for him to give to airline people, taxi drivers, and anyone else who needed to help him. With those he arrived safely in West Haven.

Even though Desmond was deaf and could hardly hear anything, the doctors told him he could hear too well to be a candidate for the implant. They gave him a stronger hearing aid, but it didn't help.

He came home discouraged. "Now what do I do?" he asked Dorothy, but she didn't know either.

The Lord was taking care of the situation, but Desmond didn't know it at the time. The Medal of Honor convention that year was held in Orange, California. It is held every two years at a different location in the United States, and airlines generously fly the Medal of Honor recipients and their wives to the conventions at no charge. So Desmond and Dorothy found themselves in southern California.

"I want to be sure to see Dot Reid while we are out there," Dorothy had told Desmond. Dot was Desmond's cousin who lived in Glendale.

They spent a little extra time in California after the convention and went to see Dot Reid. After visiting for a little while, she told them, "Some of my friends at Loma Linda have some friends who have never met Desmond, and they want to see you. Why don't we go over there this afternoon?" That was how Desmond got to Loma Linda, a large Seventh-day Adventist medical center.

The people that Desmond met were well known at the medical center, and they suggested, "Let's see if we can get you into the audiology department and have your hearing checked." Wonder of wonders they got an appointment for him the next morning.

DEAFNESS AND A COCHLEAR IMPLANT

As his hearing was being checked, Desmond asked the medical personnel, "What can you tell me about cochlear implants?"

"We are doing them here all the time now if we believe that an implant can help a person's hearing. Everyone is so different that we have to check out their hearing problems very carefully."

When they had checked out Desmond's hearing, they told him, "You are a very good candidate for the cochlear implant. Not only that, we have been talking it over and talking to the powers that be, and they have agreed to give you the cochlear implant at no cost in appreciation for your service to God and country."

Desmond could hardly believe it, but again he saw the hand of God working things out for him in such a wonderful way. However, there was one problem. The maintenance and insurance for the implant would be expensive, and the VA hadn't agreed to do anything for him on that.

Desmond and Dorothy went home, but kept working on the project. The VA kindly agreed to pay for the maintenance and insurance on the implant, so that problem was solved. But one thing they would need was money for transportation to and from California. The various military organizations in Chattanooga—the DAV, the VFW, and the Purple Heart, under the direction of Bryant Cook, head of veterans affairs—took up a donation to help them get to Loma Linda and for living expenses while they were there.

"We surely do appreciate this wonderful donation and your thoughtfulness of us and our problems," Desmond and Dorothy told them.

The donation was presented to Desmond and Dorothy at a DAV meeting. During the meeting, Desmond was called out of the meeting and found another surprise awaiting him. Dorothy's brother-in-law, Robert Jensen, handed him a key. "That's the key to my mother's house in Loma Linda. She isn't there right now, and she says you can stay in her house while you are there if you will pay the utilities and rent her small apartment for her." Desmond didn't realize what a wonderful thing this was until he got to Loma Linda and found out how much houses rented for there.

After settling into the little house only two blocks from the medical center, Desmond checked in at the audiology department. There were more tests, and more talks with Dr. Jung, who would be doing the surgery. Dr. Jung's side of the conversation, of course, was what he wrote on paper, but he was used to that.

"You see, Mr. Doss, we will go into the area behind your ear where the cochlea is. To put it in nonmedical terms, we basically connect the nerves to a magnet inside your head. Then another magnet is placed on the outside of your head at the spot where the magnet is inside your head. The sound goes by wire to a small computer you carry around in your pocket. The computer has controls on it that you can adjust as needed in order to hear."

"Do you really think it will help, Dr. Jung?" asked Desmond.

"It's hard to guarantee anything because of the complexity of ears, but I believe you have a good chance. Mr. Doss, do you believe in prayer?" asked Dr. Jung. Loma Linda is a Christian medical center, and many of the doctors are good Christians.

"Of course I do," answered Desmond, "and I surely have been praying about this. I believe God will do what is best."

Desmond's surgery was scheduled for September 1988. Thomas, Desmond and Dorothy's son, was in Hawaii at this time, and he flew to Loma Linda for his dad's surgery.

Desmond was taken to surgery. As the anesthetist was about to put him to sleep, he stopped, waited for fifteen minutes, and then started again. Then he stopped and waited a while longer.

Desmond was wondering why the operation wasn't starting, but he couldn't hear any explanation. Later he found out that just at this time something was happening that almost never happens in Loma Linda—a rainstorm with thunder and lightning. The hospital had an auxiliary electrical system, but it would take a few moments for it to kick in. The operating team didn't want anything to happen that would jeopardize Desmond's surgery.

Dorothy's brother, Dr. Harold Schutte, had a son who was a doctor and who was interning at Loma Linda Medical Center. It was comforting to Desmond to have Del in the operating room with him. Also he kept Dorothy and Thomas, who were in the waiting room, informed as to what was going on with Desmond.

Desmond woke up to a painful head and a stiff head cast. "This sure isn't very comfortable. It feels like my swelled head will pop the cast," he told Dorothy and Thomas, "but at least, I'm glad the surgery is over."

"We are, too," they both agreed.

DEAFNESS AND A COCHLEAR IMPLANT

A month later it was time to take off the cast, hook up that magnet on the outside of his head, and see how it all worked.

Linda Dyer, the very capable lady who would tune up the implant inside his head by means of the computer outside his head, carefully placed the earpiece in his ear.

"Desmond, this earpiece only holds the whole thing in place. You don't hear through it like you do with a hearing aid. Now I will place the magnet—this round piece—over the magnet in your head—you can feel it with your finger. The whole thing is already connected to the small computer that you can put in your pocket. Now, are you ready?" Linda had been writing this out for him as she talked.

"Ready as I will ever be, I guess," said Desmond.

Linda fitted the outside magnet to the inside magnet. Then she asked, "Desmond, can you hear me?"

His face lit up! "I sure can," he said. It was the first intelligible sound he had heard in twelve years.

Dorothy and Dr. Jung were watching, as well as others who were interested in what was being done. All was excitement as everyone clapped.

It wasn't finished yet. As the doctor had explained to Desmond, "This will never be as good as a hearing aid because with a hearing aid, you hear sounds you know. This gives you sounds, but they aren't sounds you are familiar with. You have to learn to recognize them as words." Desmond found this to be true.

Linda Dyer spent hours with him, teaching him and telling him how wonderful he was doing, and encouraging him in any way she could.

Even though Desmond still doesn't hear very well, it is so much better than nothing at all that he really appreciates having the cochlear implant. When he takes it off at night or his battery goes dead, he realizes even more how much he appreciates it. It is something else to thank the Lord for.

★ ★ ★ ★ ★

In June 1986 another happy incident happened. The December 1985 graduates at Southern Adventist University in Collegedale, Tennessee, asked Desmond to give their graduation address. Then in June 1986, the college decided to give Desmond an honorary degree. He and Dorothy were both dressed in a cap and gown, and he marched across the platform

DESMOND DOSS

to receive the honorary degree. He was a college graduate!

One day Dorothy was browsing at a secondhand store in Chattanooga. She noticed an eight-foot-tall replica of the Statue of Liberty.

"Desmond, I want you to go down to that secondhand store with me. You need to see something there," she told Desmond when she found him in another store.

She led the way to the Statue of Liberty replica. Desmond couldn't help but admire this symbol of his division when he was in the army. But, it was expensive, even though it was secondhand.

"Now look, Desmond," said Dorothy excitedly, "you have never smoked. You buy that statue with the smoke money you have saved." Desmond listened to his wife, and they took the statue home. Later a friend, Cliff Johnston, mounted it on a concrete pedestal.

An occasion was planned and carried out for the dedication of the Statue of Liberty. Desmond's military friends and many others came to have a part in the dedication. His Statue of Liberty still stands in Desmond's front yard, where it is a favorite spot for picture-taking.

In the center of the city of Fort Oglethorpe, Georgia, near the city of Chattanooga, Tennessee, Highway 2 crosses Route 27. From that point to Highway 193 about six miles west of the city, Highway 2 is a beautiful four-lane highway.

Bryan Hall Jackson is a likable retired military man who likes nothing better than planning nice things for heroes and other well-known men. He decided that the six miles of Highway 2 between Route 27 and Highway 193 should be named the "Desmond T. Doss Medal of Honor Highway."

On July 10, 1990, this section of highway was dedicated to Desmond.

Under the leadership of Bryan Hall Jackson, David Carroll from WRCB-TV in Chattanooga was the master of ceremonies, and Governor Joe Frank Harris of Georgia was the keynote speaker.

After the dedication ceremony, Desmond cut the ribbon, and then he and Dorothy rode from one end of the highway to the other. Desmond felt it was a great honor to have the highway named after him, the first time a highway in Georgia was named after a Medal of Honor recipient.

God has blessed Desmond so many times and in so many ways, he can't help but be thankful.

CHAPTER EIGHTEEN

TRAGEDY

The year was 1982.

"Honey, I found a lump in my breast today," Dorothy wrote to Desmond one night. "Do you suppose it might be cancer? I'm worried."

"I surely hope it isn't cancer, Sweetheart," Desmond responded. "I guess the only way to find out for sure is to go to the doctor."

Dorothy made an appointment with the doctor and a few days later received the report. It was the dreaded cancer.

Dorothy had surgery, recovered nicely, and went back to nursing.

Shortly after this, Desmond's mother also received a diagnosis of cancer, and Mother Schutte had the same diagnosis as well.

"It's an epidemic in our family, it seems," said Dorothy. "But what an awful epidemic."

Mother Doss didn't have anyone to take care of her, so Desmond decided he should go to Lynchburg to care for her. He hated to leave Dorothy, but she was doing all right in this year of 1983, and she encouraged him to go.

He spent the next six months in Lynchburg. Desmond never went home during the six months, but a few times Dorothy came to Lynchburg to see him and Mother Doss. At the end of the six months Mother Doss died. At about the same time, Mother Schutte also died.

In 1990 strange symptoms began to come to Dorothy. Was it cancer? Again Desmond and Dorothy's hopes that it wasn't were dashed. The cancer had metastasized.

DESMOND DOSS

The next year was a sad time in the Doss home. Dorothy was very brave and even cheerful, but it became evident in the summer and fall of 1991 that the cancer was taking over in her body. Worse still, the doctors couldn't promise her a complete recovery—in fact, they couldn't promise any recovery at all.

"Sweetheart, what can I do to help you not to suffer so much?" Desmond would ask as he saw her going downhill and realized she was beginning to suffer a lot.

"Massaging helps some," she would answer. So Desmond would massage her body where it hurt. Sometimes it helped. Sometimes it didn't. They both began to realize it was just a matter of time and tried not to think about the future. They prayed for God's help and blessing.

On the night of November 16, Dorothy was hurting so much. It had become routine for Desmond to massage her. But on that night it didn't seem to help much. And Desmond was so tired! But he didn't stop; he wanted to help Dorothy as much as possible while he still had her.

Finally, about 4:00 A.M., Dorothy decided to get up and take a hot bath. Maybe it would relax her. Desmond was so tired he went off to sleep as soon as she got out of bed. When she crawled back into bed, she felt better and more relaxed, and she went to sleep.

Desmond's little shaking alarm clock, made for deaf people, went off at 7:00 A.M. He could hardly pull himself out of bed, but he knew he had to get Dorothy to the hospital by 8:30 for one of the daily treatments she was receiving. He got ready to go and then wakened Dorothy.

"Sweetheart, I surely hate to wake you up, but we'll have to go if we're to get to the hospital on time. What do you want to wear?" Desmond asked.

"Just give me my coat. My dress is right here," she answered.

They got into the red Cadillac—the nicest car Desmond had ever owned. Dorothy felt it was a safe car compared with smaller ones.

As usual, they bowed their heads for prayer before leaving. "Dear Father, be with us this morning as we travel to the hospital. You know this is a time of sadness for us. Be with Dorothy. Give her comfort and strength. We ask it in Thy name. Amen," Desmond prayed.

With that, Desmond drove the car out onto the highway. Two miles down the highway was Nickajack Road, the road they would take down

TRAGEDY

Lookout Mountain to the valley. Not far from the corner was a very gentle curve, and between the curve and Nickjack Road was a ten or twelve foot drop-off on the right side of the road.

Desmond wasn't going fast, but he knew Dorothy was a little nervous so he gently touched the brake to slow the car just a little. What happened next was unbelievable! The red Cadillac went completely out of control. It skidded down the road, and then reversed direction and went over the drop-off. It landed on the passenger side of the car, crushing Dorothy's head between the roof and the seat. Dorothy was dead!

The car finally stopped upright next to a telephone pole, and the driver's side door wouldn't open against the pole. Desmond didn't believe he was hurt, but he must get out and get help! Just then the car gave another little lurch, just enough so that he could open the door. He had seen death many times during the war and since, and he knew Dorothy was dead.

"Ma'am," he said to the lady who answered the door at a nearby house, "we've had an accident. Could you please call 911 for me. I'm deaf." The little lady was so nervous she felt she couldn't call, so Desmond called 911 and asked for a rescue crew to come and bring the Jaws of Life because his wife was trapped in the car. At least he knew they could hear him—even if he couldn't hear them.

The lady agreed to call Thomas, who had come home from Hawaii to be with his mother. The police and the rescue unit arrived soon, but since Dorothy was dead, they didn't do anything until the coroner arrived. For the next two hours there was much sadness and excitement. Finally it was all over. And Desmond was without Dorothy.

The day of the funeral, it seemed the sky was sympathizing with the mourners. It rained and rained. In spite of the rain, many came to the funeral. Dorothy was loved by all. When the funeral procession reached the National Cemetery where Dorothy was to be buried, Desmond, from his place at the front of the procession, looked back from the top of the hill and saw car after car making its way to the graveside service.

Then Desmond was home with his sorrow and confusion. Because of his deafness, Dorothy had taken care of so many things, and Desmond had no idea where things were. That was hard, but mostly he missed Dorothy.

DESMOND DOSS

The next months were so hard for Desmond. He was lonely. His friends at church and at the Medal of Honor museum in Chattanooga and others were kind to him, but he felt so lost.

Losing Dorothy would have been hard under any circumstances, but with his hearing problem, it was even worse. At times he thought perhaps some day he would get married again, but he decided he would not do it for at least two years, out of respect for Dorothy and her memory. And besides, who would want to marry a deaf man?

He lived with these thoughts every day.

CHAPTER NINETEEN

HAPPINESS AGAIN

It had been a year since the accident that killed Dorothy. Desmond was beginning to feel that he needed another companion, especially after a friend reminded him that Dorothy would not want him to go on living the lonely life he was living.

One day after the fellowship dinner at church, he was talking to the pastor and his wife when the subject of his getting married again came up. Desmond said, "I need someone who can cook a decent meal. I've sure found out that I don't know how—a can of peas one day, a can of beans the next, and if I get really ambitious, a couple of potatoes with just salt. I like gravy, but I don't know how to make it. Someone who can keep a decent house would help, but any housekeeping would be an improvement over the way I've been keeping house!

"But most of all, because of my deafness, I need someone who can write out the sermons I can't hear. Oh, yes, and someone who can help me with all the mail I get."

With a chuckle, the pastor's wife said, "Desmond, you don't shop for a wife like you shop for a car."

They all laughed, but Desmond realized that, because of his deafness, he had needs that not every woman could fill.

★ ★ ★ ★ ★

Wildwood, a self-supporting institution about twenty miles down the mountain, was holding a medical seminar. Visitors from other institutions would tell good stories of God's leading when they came to the seminar.

DESMOND DOSS

On Sabbath afternoon Desmond went to Wildwood. He couldn't hear the stories very well, but after the meeting it was announced that anyone who wanted to could go on a nature walk with Earl Qualls, who knew all about nature. Desmond decided he would go.

As they hiked on the trail, Desmond saw a lady he thought looked familiar—could that possibly be Sue Westcott? He and Sue had known each other even before World War II. What was she doing at Wildwood?

Yes, it was Sue, and they had a wonderful time getting reacquainted. She told him her husband had died shortly before this, and Desmond assumed she was at Wildwood to get some help dealing with the grief she felt.

"What are you doing at Wildwood, Sue?" he asked politely, although he thought he already knew.

"Oh, I'm working here as a volunteer worker. I love it here at Wildwood. The leaders and my fellow workers are so nice. We all feel the Lord has led us here from many different directions, and it is really nice to work together as a team. I feel that this is the place where the Lord wants me to be right now," Sue answered.

At the end of the hike, Sue said to Desmond, "If you want to come down to any of the meetings at Wildwood, I'll be glad to see if I can write out what the speaker says for you."

Wonderful thought! And Desmond did take advantage of her suggestion; he found he got so much more out of the sermons than he had before. Sue was a good secretary.

As they saw each other during the weeks that followed, Desmond told Sue of his terrible loneliness during the last year.

"I really would like to get married again if I could find the companion that I feel God would want me to have."

Sue began to think of the ladies on the Wildwood campus who might be right for Desmond. She knew there were several widows—perhaps one of them would be the one.

One day she decided to phone Happy Hollow, the trailer home of two sisters—both widows. Their names were Frances Duman and Dorothy Johnson. Dorothy answered the phone. "Would either of you ladies be interested in getting acquainted with Desmond Doss? He is very lonely."

HAPPINESS AGAIN

Sue and Dorothy talked a little longer. Frances was in her room, but she was listening to Dorothy's end of the conversation—what little she could hear of it.

When Dorothy hung up, she told Frances, "Sue was wondering if either of us would be interested in getting acquainted with Desmond Doss?"

"Well, I am," Frances remarked, a little embarrassed.

At this point Frances remembered the medical seminar meetings and how one night after a meeting she was waiting in the chapel foyer to greet Bill Dull, a friend of hers who had come from Living Springs in New York. Others were talking to him, so she waited. Nearby was Desmond Doss, also waiting. When it was his turn, he and Bill enjoyed a good hug and a few words of conversation before Desmond left. As Fran watched, the thought went through her mind, *I wish I could get acquainted with him.* Perhaps now, through Sue, her wish might come true.

So it was that sometime later, Sue and Frances visited the Lookout Mountain church one Sabbath. After the fellowship dinner, Desmond took Sue and Frances to visit Margaret Miller, a church member who had had a stroke. Then they came back to the church. While Desmond and Sue visited in the pickup Desmond was driving, because his car was being fixed, Frances wandered around the grounds.

Soon it was time for them to leave. Desmond, always a gentleman, went to the other side of Sue's car and opened the door for Frances. Then around to Sue's side to open her door. But before he did, Sue turned to him and said in a soft voice, "What do you think of her?"

Suddenly he realized he was supposed to be noticing Frances—and he hadn't.

About three weeks later, Fran was the Sabbath School superintendent at the New England Adventist church in the valley near Trenton. She decided it would be nice to invite Desmond to tell his experiences as she knew he did at times. Because he is deaf and she couldn't call him, she went to his house on her afternoon off to ask him to come. He wasn't home, so she left a note. "Could you come tell your experiences at the New England Sabbath School next Sabbath?"

He called her to tell her he would come—he could talk on the phone but could not hear on it. So the arrangements were made.

Friday night it started to snow—one of those freak snowstorms in the south. By Sabbath morning there were ten to twelve inches of snow on the ground, and it snowed all day. Nobody went anywhere that day. Desmond was snowed in at his place on Lookout Mountain, and Fran and Dot were snowed in at their trailer at Wildwood. Desmond called Frances to tell her he couldn't come. She tried to explain that she wouldn't be at the New England church either, but realized he probably couldn't hear her.

Then Fran wrote him a note, "I'm sorry about the snow. Can you come next time I'm superintendent? That will be the second Sabbath in April. We have a fellowship dinner that day, and we would love to have you stay if you want to. And I'll even try to write out the sermon for you if you think I can do it." (Desmond says now that she got herself in trouble that day—offering to do just what he needed to have done. Frances doesn't agree it was trouble.)

Fran was the superintendent only once a month. Since Dot was the general superintendent, she asked Fran if someone else could have Desmond for their Sabbath School program.

"No, he's mine!" answered Fran.

Desmond answered Fran's note. "Yes, I'll be glad to come in April. After the dinner, could we go for a walk and get better acquainted? And thank you for offering to write for me—I'm sure you can do it fine."

He didn't tell Fran until much later that he wasn't even sure he would recognize her when he saw her—that's how much he had noticed her when she was at the Lookout Mountain church. But he did remember her when he saw her at the New England church.

★ ★ ★ ★ ★

Desmond had a number of friends at Wildwood, and he made a point of talking to several of them. His question was, "You know Frances Duman, of course. What kind of person is she?"

The answers from her friends were more than satisfactory. Also he knew she planned to retire in May and move to North Carolina where her son lived. He thought to himself, *I can't let her move away over to North Carolina. I might lose her. I've got to "make hay while the sun shines."*

★ ★ ★ ★ ★

Frances remembers a Sabbath when Desmond asked her to visit the Lookout Mountain church. While they were eating the fellowship dinner, Don Chace, whose wife's parents were neighbors of Fran's at Wildwood, remarked to Desmond, "She is a nice lady."

Desmond answered him, but Frances didn't hear what he said, so she asked Don, "What did he say?"

Don answered, "He said he wondered if anyone had noticed."

★ ★ ★ ★ ★

"Why don't you come down and go to prayer meeting with me?" Fran suggested.

"OK, I will," Desmond agreed.

Fran and Dot went to the New England church for prayer meeting, but Desmond didn't arrive. Where was he? They waited around for several minutes even after prayer meeting, but Desmond didn't come. Dot said, "Do you suppose he meant to meet you at the Wildwood prayer meeting?"

"I don't think so." She thought a moment. "Come to think of it, though, he might have. We really didn't specify which place." So they headed back to Wildwood. The chapel was dark, but when they went home, Desmond was there and about ready to leave. He had gone to the Wildwood prayer meeting.

They decided as they talked about this mix-up much later that the Lord had something to do with it. Because Frances wasn't with Desmond, he talked to Dr. Bernell and Dr. Marjorie Baldwin, who were friends of both Desmond and Frances. If Frances had been with him, he probably wouldn't have asked them what they thought about the romance that was developing between him and Frances. But she wasn't with him, and he did ask them what they thought. They gave him good advice and gave their blessing to the romance.

Before Desmond left Wildwood that night, he and Frances spent a few minutes talking to each other. Desmond remarked, "I haven't asked you to marry me yet."

"No, you haven't," said Frances.

"I plan to do it Friday," he said.

Frances knew Friday was the parade day in Chattanooga, a yearly parade on Armed Forces Day. Desmond was always asked to be in the parade because of his Medal of Honor. Just what did he have in mind, she wondered.

On May 14, 1993, Desmond picked Frances up at Wildwood. His dark blue pants and red coat looked very attractive on him. She was also wearing a red coat and a dark blue skirt. And both of them had happy smiles on their faces.

The parade didn't start until 1:00 P.M., but there was a dinner before that at noon. It was now only 9:00 A.M. What would happen next? Frances wondered. Desmond drove to the National Cemetery in Chattanooga and up to the top of the hill where the Medal of Honor tree was planted. Dorothy's grave was near it. The couple looked around a bit. Then . . .

"Frances, will you be my wife?" asked Desmond, as he hugged her to him.

"Yes, I will," she answered.

It felt wonderful to be officially engaged. They surely had something special to thank God for that day, and they prayed together before they left to go to the parade.

"It is wonderful to be in the parade with you, Sweetheart," said Frances. "It's the first time I have ever been in a parade. I suppose you have been in a lot of them." He agreed he had.

A cemetery is rather a queer place for a marriage proposal. But Frances thought about it and decided that Desmond probably felt one part of his life was ending and a new part starting—and that a cemetery would be a good place to start this new part of his life. She found out later that this was his thinking.

★ ★ ★ ★ ★

Desmond and Frances were looking at a 1993 calendar. What date should they set for their wedding? "My dearest," said Desmond, "I have to talk at a Baptist church in Tiftonia on July 4 and have to be in a parade in Douglasville on July 5. Why don't we get married before that so you can go with me? People always want me to go places, but I don't want to go by myself."

"Dot will be my matron of honor, and I want Mary, another sister, to be my bridesmaid. But Mary and Al are going to Washington state in June to see their son and won't be back until near the end of June. Why don't we make it Thursday, July 1? Six o'clock would probably be a good time," suggested Frances.

"I think that would be fine," said Desmond. "Since you work at Wildwood, do you think they would let us have the wedding in the chapel there? The Lookout Mountain church wouldn't be big enough. I guess we are agreed that we really do want a church wedding."

"Yes, we're agreed on that. I'm sure we can have it at Wildwood. Let's make it a simple wedding but invite everyone in the area by putting a notice in the church bulletins."

When the group was practicing for the wedding, Elder Boykin asked Desmond, just for practice, "Do you take this woman?"

To the delight of the others, Desmond answered, "I sure do!" Elder Boykin suggested that at the wedding, it might be better just to say, "I do."

Desmond and Frances were happily surprised to have about three hundred people at the wedding. "I guess they wanted to see a couple of old people get married," Frances laughingly told Desmond later.

Dot was Fran's matron of honor as planned, but Mary broke both her wrists in a fall, and Al had to have surgery, so they couldn't come. Fran asked her daughter-in-law, Tracy, to fill in. Desmond's best man was Bob Jensen, his brother-in-law, and his groomsman was Dr. Bernell Baldwin. The flower girl and Bible boy were Heidi and Paul Hogfeldt, children of Fran's co-worker in the accounting office. Elder Bill Boykin performed the ceremony. Loretta Wilson made sure everyone in the wedding party did what they should when they should, and Sue was there to remind Frances as she started up the aisle, "Be sure to smile. This is a happy day."

Standing at the back of the chapel and waiting for her cue to go down the aisle, Frances looked to the platform where Desmond was already in his place. What a thrill to be marrying her Desmond! Later she asked Desmond what he was thinking about right then. "Just wondering if I could do everything right." He did.

Beautiful music was provided by Margaret on her violin; Lorraine, Fran's friend from Florida, sang "Because," and a trio of Dona, Anita, and Roby Ann sang a song Warren Wilson had written, "Jesus and You and I."

It wasn't easy to find a big enough place to have the reception, so Frances wanted to have it out on the lawn near the Wildwood chapel. Thursday morning it was hard to tell whether it might rain later on. Someone suggested that they have the reception in the new store building. It had been finished but didn't have the shelves and furniture in it. Besides it was air-conditioned, and the afternoon turned out to be hot and humid. Jeannette Atwood, the store manager, graciously gave her consent, and Diane McInnis and her helpers moved in to set up. Laurel Rudnick baked and decorated the beautiful five-tiered fruit cake. When it came time to cut the cake, Desmond remembers that he started to saw on it. It started to wiggle from side to side, so he stopped in time to avert disaster. It was a lovely reception.

After the wedding, the couple spent the first three days in a nice wedding motel—their own home on Lookout Mountain. It was away back off the highway and was quiet and peaceful. What could be better!

On Sunday and Monday they kept the appointments Desmond had. Then they were on their own. They enjoyed spending a few days in Helen, Georgia, a quaint European-style village. Frances showed her "stupidity" there. She took twenty-four pictures without film in the camera. (Guess what: She did the same thing three years later when they spent their third anniversary there.) But for their honeymoon, they went to North Carolina for the weekend with their son Mike, his wife Tracy, and their two boys, Christopher and Jonathon.

The whole courtship and marriage seemed like a dream, even a miracle, as they remembered how God had brought them together. The years have been kind to the Dosses, and they thank the Lord every day for the happiness He has brought to them.

★ ★ ★ ★ ★

Even though it has been more than fifty years since Desmond received the Medal of Honor, he still receives many requests for autographs, and he is asked to speak at churches, schools, and other meetings quite often. He is thankful that he can do this to encourage others in their walk with the Lord.

CHAPTER TWENTY

ONCE MORE IN OKINAWA

In March 1995, Desmond received a form letter from John Mandeville, head of the U.S. Army on Okinawa, inviting Okinawa veterans to return to the island for the fiftieth anniversary of the World War II victory over Japan. The celebration was also to commemorate fifty years of peace and friendship between America and Japan.

Desmond answered the letter. He mentioned he held the Medal of Honor. As soon as John Mandeville learned that, Desmond and Frances began receiving phone calls from Okinawa. The army wanted him to be there for the celebration—especially since he had received the Medal of Honor for what he did on Okinawa.

The army agreed to pay Desmond's travel expenses, and since because of his deafness he wouldn't be able to go without Frances, the army agreed to pay her expenses, too.

Dennis Johnson, a missionary inhalation therapist at the Hong Kong Adventist Hospital, was a friend of the Dosses. He had been at their home the summer before, and Frances had said to him, "When you get to Hong Kong, we'll come to see you." They all laughed because they knew how impossible that would be.

But now Frances said, "We just have to go to Hong Kong to see Dennis." They did go to Hong Kong before going to Okinawa. Dennis and his friend Hazel (they were married the next June) showed them around while they were there. They took the bus to the highest spot in Hong Kong and enjoyed the view. Another day they went to the Chinese marketplace—a most interesting excursion. On Sabbath they all went to church, which was held in the chapel of the hospital building. In the afternoon Desmond spoke to the Philippine Adventist believers. Afterward they all wanted pictures, so Desmond and Frances stood in the center while various groups moved in for pictures, and then moved out so another group could move in.

On Sunday Desmond and Frances flew to Okinawa. John Mandeville and his wife were there to meet them, as well as Bryan and Mischelle Canter. John Mandeville had learned that Desmond and Frances were Seventh-day Adventists, and he thoughtfully assigned Captain Bryan Canter, a Seventh-day Adventist, to be Desmond's escort while he was on Okinawa.

"We've made arrangements for you to stay at the Kadeena Air Force Base. But would you like to see the Adventist church on the way out there?" asked Bryan.

"Yes, of course," both agreed. So they saw the International Seventh-day Adventist church on that first evening on Okinawa. Desmond remembered it. He had been on Okinawa during World War II, of course, but he had been there also in 1969. At that time the church had just finished a building for a serviceman's center next to the church itself.

"Do you know, Bryan," Desmond said, "I was the first one to sleep in the serviceman's center? You see, I was here in 1969 when the center was dedicated. I asked if I could sleep there the first night, and they let me."

Later Bryan told Desmond, "You will need to go to certain functions while you are here on Okinawa, Desmond, but at other times we can go off on our own and see what we want to see. I'm at your service."

One day they went to a place where there is a wall, like the one in Washington, D.C., that lists the names of those who were killed. Another day they had quite an adventure in getting to Ie Shima, where Ernie Pyle, the famous war correspondent, was killed. Mischelle went along that day. The plan was to take a ferry and go with the whole group to the island. They drove to the area where the ferry was supposed to be—and couldn't find it! Most of the people in that part of Okinawa did not know how to speak English, so Bryan had to look for someone who could speak English and who knew the area. He finally found someone who could tell him how to get to the ferry, and they drove to the dock—only to see the ferry pull out into the ocean!

ONCE MORE IN OKINAWA

Poor Bryan. He felt so bad. But another ferry would leave in an hour. The foursome were on that one. They got to Ie Shima. Now what?

Again Bryan went to ask questions. While he was gone, a soldier asked the others, "Where do you want to go?"

"We were supposed to be here for the ceremony at the Ernie Pyle monument, but we missed the ferry. Now we need to go to the monument, even though we're late," they answered.

"I'll take you there in my army van," he offered. So they did get to the interesting monument, took some pictures, and got back to the ferry in time to go back to Okinawa with the whole group, which had been touring the island.

Another day was a most interesting and pleasurable one. They were to go to Zamami Shima, another island. And they were to go by helicopter! They arrived at the place where they were to board the helicopter, checked in, and were fitted with life jackets (they were flying over the ocean) and ear phones to hear any instructions.

They loved that, especially Frances. It was her first time on a helicopter. On the island, a Japanese-American ceremony was held to dedicate a monument, and then they went up the hill where they could overlook the ocean and see Zamami Village.

While they were eating the lunch supplied by the army, Desmond discovered his little microphone that helped him hear people at close range was gone. Bryan and a friend went to see if they could find it, while Desmond and Frances walked on the beach and prayed it would be recovered. When Bryan returned, he had the microphone! The helicopter pilot found it near the helicopter, but didn't know whom it belonged to. Frances and Desmond remembered to thank God.

Bryan took Desmond and Frances to the Battle of Okinawa Museum, three rooms of mementos collected by Dave Davenport. When Bryan introduced Desmond, Dave's face lit up. "I've taken people up on the escarpment many times, and I always tell them the story of Desmond Doss. I'm so thrilled to have you here," he said.

After a day of sightseeing, Desmond and Frances and Bryan and Mischelle would come back to the Canter's home for a lovely dinner. Mischelle would invite different families from the church to eat with them and meet Desmond. They enjoyed it immensely.

DESMOND DOSS

On Friday evening Mischelle invited the church elder, Mr. Rice, and his wife and family. Their daughter was thirteen or fourteen years old, and she had beautiful, long, shiny, black hair—so long it hung below her waist. Desmond said to her, "Don't ever cut your hair. It is so pretty. I used to braid my mother's hair for her. She had long hair, too, but not as long as yours."

Then he took her hair in his hands and started to braid it very loosely. He soon let it out, and it went back to its original long, black, shiny condition. Next day she told a friend, "Desmond Doss braided my hair last night. I'm never going to wash it again."

On Sabbath, Bryan and Mischelle took Desmond and Frances to church. It was an interesting service. Dean Horonouchi, the minister who was from America, preached the sermon. He told Desmond's story as part of his sermon. The ladies of the church served a lovely fellowship dinner, and the whole group was very friendly to their visitors.

Desmond and Frances went through the line and sat down at one of the tables. Soon a little girl, about five or six years old, sat down beside Desmond. Frances noticed that she had a small serving of spaghetti on her paper plate and nothing else. But her small dessert plate was heaped with every kind of dessert she could squeeze onto the plate.

Then she looked up at Desmond with adoring eyes, and said, "You can have some, too. There's a lot there," as she pointed to the table. How could they keep from laughing?

There was a monument in front of the church to the soldiers who fought on Okinawa. It mentioned Desmond by name. There had once been a monument dedicated to Desmond Doss near the escarpment. But after it became surrounded by buildings and grown up with weeds, it was decided to bring the big monument down to the church yard. So now it was in the front yard of the church.

At the end of the week-long celebration of the fiftieth anniversary of the war's end, Bryan had to go back to work at the base, but the Dosses' plane was not scheduled to leave for three days. So the Dosses were taken to other lovely places on Okinawa by Dean and Kathy Horonouchi and Andrew and Deanne. They remember one evening when they ate at Kathy's table—with chopsticks. A lot of laughing was done.

Desmond remembers another incident on Okinawa. He likes to ask people, "Have you ever been bitten by a fish?" He goes on to explain,

ONCE MORE IN OKINAWA

"The Horonouchis took us to the ocean one day. We went out on the ocean in a glass-bottomed boat. The captain of the little boat passed out a kind of bread to feed the fish. I reached over the side of the boat with a piece of this bread in my hand. Two big fish tried to eat it. One got the bread; the other got my finger."

★ ★ ★ ★ ★

Before returning to the United States, Desmond and Frances spent a wonderful four days on Guam. Desmond had been on Guam with the army back in 1944.

The Seventh-day Adventist people on Guam were happy to welcome them. Fran's nephew and family, Calvin and Laura Rick, Bonnie, and Albert, had been missionaries there for several years when Calvin was a doctor at the Adventist clinic. Mary (Fran's sister) and Al Rick were teachers there for a time also.

One place on Guam that they visited was Adventist World Radio (AWR), which preaches the gospel over the radio in that part of the world. That was a thrilling visit.

★ ★ ★ ★ ★

Desmond and Frances have made some changes in their lives recently. Instead of living on Lookout Mountain near Chattanooga, Tennessee, they have moved to Piedmont, Alabama where they live near their son and his wife, Michael and Tracy Duman. Since Desmond has become nearly blind in recent months, they do not accept any speaking engagements, but stay at home. They are very happy in their present surroundings, but are looking forward to the coming of their precious Lord and Savior, Jesus Christ.

★ ★ ★ ★ ★

As Desmond Doss looks back over the many years of his life, he can't help but remember, sometimes with amazement, but always with thankfulness, how the great God of the universe has taken care of him.

CHAPTER TWENTY-ONE

CANCER

"Sweetheart, I haven't been feeling very well, and I seem to be having urination problems," Desmond confided to Frances one day in 1999. Actually he had been having such troubles for some time. Frances's son, Michael Duman, is an anesthetist and works in Rome, Georgia.

"Mom, why don't you bring Dad down here to Rome to see Dr. Formby? He is a urologist and very good. Let Dr. Formby see what he thinks about it," Mike suggested over the phone one day.

"That sounds like a good idea—if Desmond will do it," answered Frances. Desmond thought it was a good idea, too, and on June 22, they were in the doctor's office.

The doctor talked to Desmond. He thought Desmond might be having some spasms, but he needed to find out for sure. "I will really need to take a biopsy," he told them.

"How soon, Dr. Formby?" asked Frances.

"How about tomorrow?" he answered.

So the next morning found Desmond in the outpatient department at the hospital. Mike came in to see Desmond for a moment. He said to him, "A problem came up with your blood test this morning. Your hemoglobin is very low."

"What does that mean?" Desmond and Frances asked.

"You will have to wait and see what Dr. Formby says," he answered.

Moments later Dr. Formby arrived, repeating Mike's information. "We will need to give you a blood transfusion and then put off the biopsy for a few days. It would be dangerous to put you to sleep when your hemoglobin is so low." So Desmond received three pints of blood and an antibiotic that day.

A few days later Desmond had the biopsy. Frances waited in the waiting room until her name was called. Dr. Formby met her in the hall.

"Mrs. Doss," he reported to her, "it is cancer in his bladder. Now he will need to have a CAT scan to see if and how far it has spread."

Arrangements were soon made, and Desmond found himself in another building, lying on a hard table and being electrically pushed in and out of a small enclosed section of the room while X-rays were being taken of his bladder. The CAT scan confirmed the cancer in his bladder, but it had not metastasized to any other organ.

Later Mike told Desmond and Frances, "Dr. Formby was very much surprised to find that the cancer was only in the bladder because that kind of cancer would usually metastasize from another organ to the bladder."

What next?

Desmond—and Frances, too—felt the need for special prayer for Desmond, so one day they stopped at the conference office. The group there gathered around Desmond and prayed for his healing. That was a source of real encouragement to him.

Another time a special time of prayer was held at Desmond's home. He and Frances remembered that in the book of James in the Bible, it says that when a person is sick, he should call for the elders and that they should pray for the sick person and anoint him with oil and that the prayer of faith would save the sick. So one day Elder John Swafford, Elder Allan Williamson, and Elder Les Rilea came to Desmond's home on Lookout Mountain and followed those directions. It was a wonderful service.

But from a medical standpoint, the doctor felt Desmond should have treatments for his bladder cancer. Desmond and Frances believe that God gives doctors knowledge and skill to treat many diseases, cancer being one of them. So every Tuesday for the next six weeks Desmond had a treatment in which a substance that would kill the cancer was inserted into the bladder and held there for a time.

Every time Desmond had a treatment, the side effects would be a little more uncomfortable. He would have a certain amount of nausea and just didn't feel good. He also had a high fever at times and felt very weak.

And thereby hangs a wonderful miracle! Watch as it unfolds.

DESMOND DOSS

★ ★ ★ ★ ★

The big international Pathfinder camporee was to be held at Oshkosh, Wisconsin, on August 10–14. John Swafford, the leader of the young people in the Georgia-Cumberland Conference of Seventh-day Adventists, is a good friend of Desmond and Frances, and he always likes to have Desmond at Pathfinder camporees.

"Frances, we hope you and Desmond can come to the Oshkosh camporee. It is always an inspiration for the young people to have Desmond there. Can you plan to come?" John asked over the phone.

"I'm not sure, John. You know Desmond is taking these treatments for his cancer. He surely would like to come, I know, but we'll have to wait and see how he feels by then. We'll keep in touch," Frances answered. Since Desmond is deaf, he doesn't talk over the telephone, so Frances has to substitute.

One time when he was at the doctor's office, Desmond said, "Dr. Formby, we have this opportunity to go to Wisconsin for a young people's camp, but it comes during the week of my last treatment. Would it be all right if I took that treatment next week?"

Dr. Formby answered, "That would be all right—if you feel like going." So Desmond planned to go.

Time went fast, and soon it was the week before the planned trip to Wisconsin. Fran's sister, Dorothy Johnson, planned to go, too, to help drive and to see her son and family who lived in Jefferson, not far from Oshkosh.

It was Thursday, the week before the camp was to open on Tuesday, August 10. "Sweetheart, I don't feel good at all. The treatment this week has really knocked me out," Desmond told Frances. "I don't feel we should try to go to Wisconsin, much as I want to. If we got up there, and I got sick, it wouldn't be so good." So they decided it would be best to stay home.

Frances knew how much Desmond really wanted to go. He always enjoyed being with the Pathfinders, and this was a very special camporee. But what else could they do?

The weekend passed, and by Sunday afternoon Desmond was feeling a little better—really a lot better. He decided maybe he could take the trip as planned. It was too late to drive, but John had offered to fly them to

CANCER

Wisconsin. Besides, Dorothy found her children planned to be gone that week, so there wasn't much reason for her to go.

So Monday morning Frances made some phone calls. Yes, they could fly to Appleton, Wisconsin, the closest airport to Oshkosh. But there was a big problem. Desmond and Frances would need to be met at Appleton, and because there was no answer on that line, Frances couldn't get to John Swafford to have him make arrangements to meet them. So, once again, they decided there was only one thing to do—stay home.

"Sweetheart, since we aren't going to Wisconsin as planned, do you think I should go ahead and have that last treatment, even though the doctor said I could wait?" Desmond asked Frances on Monday night.

"Yes, I think you should do it and get it over with," agreed Frances.

So the next day Desmond went to the outpatient department again for his last treatment.

The first part of the miracle—he didn't get sick like he usually did.

Wednesday morning at about 9:00 A.M. the phone rang, and Frances answered it. It was John Swafford at the camp in Oshkosh. He had just heard through his office in Calhoun, Georgia, that Desmond wasn't planning to come to the camporee.

"Frances, how is Desmond doing? Do you think he could possibly make it to the camporee? We really want him to come. We have him on the program for tonight, and we and the Pathfinders will miss him if he isn't here."

"John, I tried to make arrangements on Monday to fly up there Tuesday but couldn't get you on the phone so that you could have someone meet us. Desmond had his last treatment yesterday, but I'll ask him and see what he says," offered Frances.

So she went to talk to Desmond. "Honey, this is John on the phone. He wants to know if you can possibly fly up to Oshkosh today if they can make the arrangements."

"YES!"

So back to the phone Frances went and relayed the message. A half hour later John and Fred Fuller were on the phone again. "All arrangements are made. You can catch the plane at Chattanooga at 12:30, change planes in Cincinnati, and arrive at Appleton around 5:00 P.M. Fred Fuller will meet you and bring you to the camp."

DESMOND DOSS

It was 9:30 A.M. and they would need to be at the airport in Chattanooga, a forty-five-minute drive away, by 11:30 A.M. Can you imagine what happened in the Doss household during the next hour and fifteen minutes? But they were on the plane at 12:30, and they thanked the Lord.

Fred Fuller met them and took them to the motel and then to the camp, where there was food in the office area. They were waiting behind the big platform when the evening program started. It was unbelievable that they were really there!

Now it was time for Desmond Doss to go on the platform. His story of receiving the Congressional Medal of Honor for letting approximately seventy-five men over a cliff and down about thirty-five feet to where they could be taken on down to the aid station for care was told to the 22,000 boys and girls and counselors who had assembled that night.

Then there was a complete and wonderful surprise for Desmond. On the platform with Desmond and Frances were Pathfinder leaders John Swafford and Fred Fuller from the Georgia-Cumberland Conference of Seventh-day Adventists, Allan Williamson from the Southern Union Conference, and Willie Oliver, from the North American Division, as well as several other leaders. "Desmond Doss, you have worked with Pathfinders, spent time with them at camporees, talked to them many times, and you have wished at times that you were a Master Guide. Tonight we are going to make that wish come true." Then, as he put the Master Guide scarf around Desmond's neck, Allan said, "You are now a Master Guide. Congratulations!" (Desmond found out later that the Master Guide scarf Allan Williamson put around his neck actually belonged to Allan himself because they didn't have an extra one for Desmond. That made it even more precious to Desmond.)

What a happy surprise for Desmond. As he accepted the honor, he said, "This is the best honor I have had in my life. It's even better than a Medal of Honor."

The next Sabbath it was Desmond's happy privilege to invest two others who were becoming Master Guides. And Frances even invested one girl. It was a happy time.

The Three Angels Broadcasting Network (3ABN), located in southern Illinois, was at the camp with video equipment. Desmond's whole

CANCER

ceremony was recorded to play on 3ABN's satellite station. Desmond has a video of that evening's program.

Thursday, Friday, and Sabbath were wonderful days for Desmond and Frances. Glenda Patterson, Elizabeth Tucker, and Carol Elliott drove them all over the campgrounds in the golf carts or in a car if they went off the campgrounds. Desmond talked to groups of Pathfinders a couple of times and then signed his new book, Desmond Doss in God's Care. Every place he went the boys and girls wanted autographs or just wanted to shake his hand or talk to him.

He was in the parades, or watching them, as the Pathfinders marched down the main road of the camp to where they could watch airplanes doing stunts. On Sabbath he and Frances were in the parade in Oshkosh that showed the good effects of avoiding alcohol and drugs.

Now for the second part of the miracle: after his treatments, the usual pattern had been nausea, fever, and weakness for several days. During the time at camp, even though Desmond had just had his treatment on Tuesday, he felt remarkably well. His stomach felt just a little queasy at times, and he found that tomato juice helped, so the staff saw to it that he had tomato juice to drink whenever he wanted it. His appetite was good, and he enjoyed the food.

Sunday morning the 1999 Pathfinder Camporee was over and it was time to pack up and go home. The faithful Fred Fuller again used his car to take Desmond and Frances to the airport in Appleton, and by that afternoon they were back in Chattanooga, Tennessee. Desmond jumped in their car and drove to a nearby gas station to fill the car with gas. But Frances could tell he was not feeling well at all, so while he was getting gas she moved over into the driver's seat and drove the rest of the way home.

When they arrived home, Desmond said, "I feel rotten," and "he hit the bed," as Frances expressed it. For two days his stomach refused to keep anything down, and the next two days were nearly as bad. The next two days he spent in the hospital, and he really didn't feel good for about two weeks.

That is the reason Desmond and Frances say the Oshkosh camporee was a miracle for Desmond. During the four days they were at the camporee, as well as traveling there and back, Desmond felt good, ate well, enjoyed being with the young people, autographed books, was in parades, and did many things. But when he arrived home, he was sick and felt worse than he usually felt after a treatment. Why did he feel good, why did he eat well, why did he not get sick at camp? They feel it was because God performed a miracle for him.

Of course, the doctors are following Desmond's cancer. In September 1999, the results of the biopsy were negative, but in December, the results had turned positive again.

So in February and March of 2000, Desmond had thirty radiation treatments. In June when he was checked again, the results were negative. He was able to be active and work more than he had in a long time and didn't get as tired as he used to.

On the day that Desmond received the last negative report, he was so happy that he decided to stop by the Georgia-Cumberland Conference office in Calhoun again. He wanted to tell John and the others the good news. Before they left the office that day, Desmond and Frances—together with John, his secretary, Glenda, and others—knelt and thanked God for His care for Desmond and for the good medical report.

God has taken care of Desmond, and he wants to give his own testimony. The following is his testimony:

Message from Desmond Doss
July 2000

I want to say that being made a Master Guide at the Pathfinder camporee in Oshkosh, Wisconsin, was the greatest honor of my life. To me, it represents the great love I have for young people. The Master Guide was given to me before 22,000 young people at the camporee, and I have the video of the program that was made by 3ABN.

Now to my cancer experience.

In June 1999, I found out I had bladder cancer. At one time I got so sick and so weak I could not stand up or walk. Twice when we went to the doctor's office Frances had to get a wheelchair from his office to wheel me in. When I was so sick and so weak and couldn't keep food on my stomach, I began to wonder, How long can I last?

At that time I was so thankful for the "blessed hope" of our

CANCER

Lord's soon return. I felt prepared to go to sleep in Jesus. I had been anointed and prayed for according to the Bible instruction in James 5:14 by Elders John Swafford, Allan Williamson, and Les Rilea, longtime friends of mine. We did not necessarily ask for God's healing. It was God's will that we wanted done. I was greatly comforted in believing that God knows what is best. If it were God's will that I should rest until Jesus comes, that was all right with me.

It is a blessing to know that, if I die, I will be called from my grave when Jesus comes and that I will have a perfect body and perfect health to serve Him with. Also, I can be with Christ and loved ones and friends through all eternity.

The Bible tells us in 1 Corinthians 2:9, "Eye hath not seen, nor ear heard, neither have entered into the heart of man, the things which God hath prepared for them that love him." The Bible also says in John 14:15: "If ye love me, keep my commandments." Because I love God and Christ with all my heart, I have always tried to keep his Ten Commandments. The principles of the commandments are included in the Golden Rule, and I feel that I received the Congressional Medal of Honor because of the love God gave me for my fellow men. I put them before myself. I enjoy helping people.

Back to the cancer again. The last biopsy I had showed no cancer. Knowing God saw best to heal me of my cancer, I want to be used of Him to help others to love Jesus with all of their hearts also.

Sincerely,
Desmond T. Doss

Looking down a shaft from the top of the escarpment where the Japanese crawled up and down on ladders.

Desmond Doss on top of the Maeda Escarpment on Okinawa. It was at this place where Desmond prayed for the soldiers and none were killed and only one man hurt—by a rock that hit his hand. The rope in the picture was the one used to lower approximately seventy-five wounded men down the cliff the next day.

Desmond and Dorothy Doss on their wedding day, August 17, 1942.

Honorary Degree

Desmond and Dorothy Doss at Southern College of Seventh-day Adventists May 2–4, 1986. Desmond received an honorary degree at that time.

The Doss family on the 50th wedding anniversary of the parents. Left to Right are Harold and Hilda Doss, Audrey and Lawson Millner, and Dorothy and Desmond Doss. The parents are in front.

Desmond Doss on the Maeda Escarpment in 1995. The top of the escarpment is now a beautiful Japanese memorial park. This is the spot on the escarpment where Desmond let the men down the cliff.

Desmond giving one of the many talks he gives about Okinawa and other war areas in World War II. Here he is demonstrating tying the bowline knot which he used to lower the men off the escarpment.

Desmond and Frances Doss riding the helicopter to Zamami Shima. It was a fun trip for a happy couple.

Desmond "tying up" John Swafford, Youth Ministries leader of the Georgia-Cumberland Conference of Seventh-day Adventists at a Pathfinder Camporee at Cohutta Springs, Georgia. Picture taken April 18, 1998.

Below: Desmond and Frances in Pathfinder uniforms. Desmond has told his story to thousands of young pathfinders.

The Lookout Mountain Seventh-day Adventist Church which Desmond helped to build.

This highway was named after Desmond T. Doss in Ft. Oglethorpe, Georgia. Dedicated July 10, 1990.

The mountain home of Desmond and Frances Doss on Lookout Mountain in Georgia, but near Chatta- nooga, Tennessee. Note the flag and the Statue of Liberty in the front yard. Bottom: Snow at Desmond's house in March 1993.

*Desmond and Frances Doss
at home in 1997. (Photo by
Dr. Jim Coy used by
permission.)*

*Desmond and Frances
Doss September 1, 2005*

p 12 Coin, murder,
pacificism